Scottish Philosophy of Rhetoric

By Rosaleen Keefe

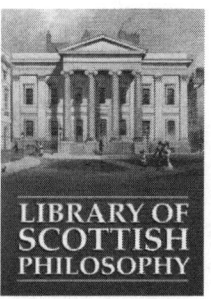

IMPRINT ACADEMIC

Copyright © Rosaleen Keefe, 2014

The moral rights of the author have been asserted.
No part of this publication may be reproduced in any form
without permission, except for the quotation of brief passages
in criticism and discussion.

Published in the UK by Imprint Academic
PO Box 200, Exeter EX5 5YX, UK

Distributed in the USA by
Ingram Book Company,
One Ingram Blvd., La Vergne, TN 37086, USA

ISBN 9781845405618

A CIP catalogue record for this book is available from the
British Library and US Library of Congress

Full series details:

www.imprint-academic.com/losp

Contents

Series Editor Note	v
Introduction	1
1. Francis Hutcheson (1694–1746)	22
Reading I: *Inquiry into the Original of Our Ideas of Beauty and Virtue*	24
Reading II: *System of Moral Philosophy in Three Parts*	31
2. Henry Homes, Lord Kames (1696–1782)	42
Reading III: *Elements of Criticism*	44
3. Adam Smith (1723–1790)	52
Readings IV, V, VI, and VII: *Lectures on Rhetoric and Belles Lettres (1762–63)*	55
4. Alexander Gerard (1728–1795)	88
Readings VIII and IX: *Essay on Taste*	90
5. Thomas Reid (1710–1796)	99
Reading X: *Essays on the Intellectual and Active Powers of Man*	101
Reading XI and XII: *Inquiry into the Human Mind Upon the Principles of Common Sense*	104
6. George Campbell (1719–1796)	111
Reading XIII, XIV and XV: *The Philosophy of Rhetoric*	113
7. Hugh Blair (1718–1800)	139
Reading XVI, XVII and XVIII: *Lectures on Rhetoric and Belles Lettres*	141
8. Alexander Bain (1818–1903)	179
Reading XIX: *English Composition and Rhetoric*	181
Index of Names	189

Series Editor's Note

The principal purpose of volumes in this series is not to provide scholars with accurate editions, but to make the writings of Scottish philosophers accessible to a new generation of modern readers in an attractively produced and competitively priced format. In accordance with this purpose, certain changes have been made to the original texts:
- Spelling and punctuation have been modernized.
- In some cases the selections have been given new titles.
- Some original footnotes and references have not been included.
- Some extracts have been shortened from their original length.
- Quotations from Greek have been transliterated, and passages in languages other than English translated, or omitted altogether.

Care has been taken to ensure that in no instance do these amendments truncate the argument or alter the meaning intended by the original author. For readers who want to consult the original texts, full bibliographical details are provided for each extract.

The Library of Scottish Philosophy was originally an initiative of the Centre for the Study of Scottish Philosophy at the University of Aberdeen. The first six volumes, published in 2004, were commissioned with financial support from the Carnegie Trust for the Universities of Scotland. In 2006 the CSSP moved to Princeton where it became one of three research centers within the Special Collections of Princeton Theological Seminary Library, and with the Seminary's financial support more volumes have been published.

Scottish Philosophy of Rhetoric is the fifteenth volume in the series and has been prepared for publication by Alexander Peterson.

Acknowledgements

The CSSP gratefully acknowledges financial support from the Carnegie Trust and Princeton Theological Seminary, the enthusiasm and excellent service of the publisher *Imprint Academic*, and the permission of the University of Aberdeen Special Collections and Libraries to use the engraving of the Faculty of Advocates (1829) as the logo for the series.

Gordon Graham,
Princeton, October 2013

Rosaleen Keefe

Introduction

Scottish Rhetoric and Scottish Philosophy

The Scottish contribution to the creation of modern Western institutions is one of the most surprising chapters in the history of modernity. It is counterintuitive to suppose that such a small and low profile country should be the source of philosophical innovations that forged the conceptual foundations of political, social, psychological, educational, and economic systems still functioning today. It may also seem counterintuitive to regard the oft-forgotten discipline of rhetoric as central to the philosophical practice that produced these foundations. So in imagining a volume on the *Scottish Philosophy of Rhetoric*, it may appear overambitious to link the Scottish philosophical tradition to the Scottish rhetorical texts so closely, especially since the Enlightenment rhetorical tradition, particularly when viewed from the perspective of writing and reading pedagogy, is often seen as simply an obtuse and dated addendum to the main philosophical tradition.

On the other hand, within rhetorical history, the eighteenth century is widely regarded as the central nexus of the development of many modern conversations about language, language-learning, social and cognitive development through language, semantics, linguistics, discourse theory, and civic participation. Further, any consideration of eighteenth- and nineteenth-century rhetoric must focus on the contributions of Scottish writers and professors such as George Campbell and Hugh Blair. The selections in this volume have been chosen in order to show readers both why the Scottish contributions to rhetoric are important for those conversations, and also how essential their place is in the Scottish philosophical tradition.

To *whom* amongst the many eminent Scottish Enlightenment thinkers should we look first for the key texts of Scottish rhetoric? Rhetoric, though a subject of widespread interest at that time, is hard to confine within any one discipline, as indeed it continues to be. Linda Ferreira-Buckley, describing the broad state of eighteenth-century rhetoric, points out that 'then, as now, "rhetoric" is an expansive phenomenon and a slippery term. Understanding the eighteenth-century requires looking beyond disciplinary boundaries that may have come to seem natural'.[1] The arguments regarding aesthetics, epistemology, and the ontology of perception, philosophy of mind, and logic put forward by Francis Hutcheson, Alexander Gerard, Lord Kames, and Thomas Reid in response to the innovations in philosophy, logic, and method that were made by Bacon, Newton, Locke, and Berkeley are now fixed parts of the philosophical context. But while the Scottish philosophers themselves considered rhetorical inquiry and teaching central to their own work, their ideas on rhetoric and language were developed even further by their students, Campbell and Blair (and several decades later, Alexander Bain), all of whom wrote rhetorical theory and textbooks that influenced generations of language learners on several continents. Often, these texts are taken to represent only the Scottish rhetorical tradition, but they have an equally important role in the philosophy of language.

The selections in this volume comprise a unique introduction to Scottish rhetorical innovations that have generally been overlooked in studies of the philosophical tradition, while at the same time being used to oversimplify the rhetorical tradition. This volume is the first of its kind to choose texts in such a way as to demonstrate, and not simply refer to, these essential connections between Scottish philosophy and Scottish rhetoric. Organized loosely by biographic and bibliographic succession, the aim is to exhibit the variety and vigour of Scottish rhetorical thinking, while

---

[1] Ferreira-Buckley, Linda, 'The Eighteenth Century', in *The Present State of Scholarship in the History of Rhetoric,* Columbia: University of Missouri Press, 2010.

placing it within the broader conceptual structure developed and articulated by George Campbell and Hugh Blair. It requires some flexibility on the part of the reader to examine philosophical texts for their rhetorical theory, and at the same time read pedagogical texts for their underlying philosophy of language. Only in this way, however, do we arrive at a more complete picture of Scottish rhetoric, as a vibrant and resonant body of rhetorical theory and practice. It is my hope that a reader from any discipline, not only those interested in Scottish philosophy or rhetorical theory, will gain a new comprehension of the centrality of the Scottish rhetorical tradition to these topics.

Rhetoric and Logic in Eighteenth-Century Scotland

In the classical tradition, rhetoric is one of the three cornerstones of a basic education in the liberal arts, the *trivium*, which consisted of logic, rhetoric, and grammar. The study of rhetoric, defined by Aristotle as the 'ability to see, in each particular case, the means of persuasion',[2] was since ancient times considered a first order in education; it is easy to see how along with grammar, the basic means for forming intelligible units of speech, and logic, the art of constructing rationally valid arguments, these three together create a fitting foundation to intellectual inquiry. All of the authors included in this volume would have had a thorough background in the history and practice of rhetoric and logic. The relationship of logic to rhetoric is of particular importance to the development of what Wilbur Samuel Howell, in his seminal histories of eighteenth-century logic and rhetoric,[3]

---

[2] Aristotle, *On Rhetoric*, translated by George Kennedy, Oxford: Oxford University Press, 1991, 2.1, p. 36. Kennedy notes that Aristotle defines rhetoric into the genus of *dynamis*, or 'potentiality', indicating that rhetoric is the not the product of speech or writing, it is the 'art of "seeing" how persuasion may be effected' (p. 36, footnote 34). This is an important distinction, relative to the Scottish philosophy of rhetoric as well. The art of rhetoric must not be confused with the products of rhetorical arts.

[3] Howell, Wilbur Samuel, *Eighteenth-Century British Logic and Rhetoric*, Princeton: Princeton University Press, 1971; and *Logic and Rhetoric in England, 1500–1700*, Princeton: Princeton University Press, 1956.

termed the 'new rhetoric' of Enlightenment thinkers, and it is also crucial to understanding the rhetorical innovations of the Scottish Enlightenment.

Logic had undergone a transformation since the works of Francis Bacon, who persuasively condemned the classical Aristotelian syllogism as an insufficient tool for genuine scientific inquiry. Bacon argued that science required a logical form that allowed for observation and inquiry, and that syllogism and the art of deduction could only form arguments from what is, essentially, already known. A new logic of induction was necessary for the new scientific method. This inductive method relies not on *a priori* knowledge, but rather on observation of particulars, and probabilities of generalities. The discipline of logic, therefore, needed to be reformed. Now, Alexander Broadie argues that 'in the forefront of this discussion on logic in the mid-eighteenth century' and 'pressing for debate toward further modernization of the discipline'[4] was none other than Thomas Reid. Reid is much better known for his development of Scottish Common Sense philosophy, dealing with the more abstract branches of epistemology and philosophy of mind, but it is important to note that, like many of the thinkers included here for their important work in rhetorical theory, he was as well-versed in science and mathematics as in philosophical inquiry. This is essential to understanding the motivation for the rhetorical innovations he, like others, advocated. In fact, the relation of logic to rhetoric and the concern with science is essential to understanding the particularly Scottish Enlightenment crafting of the 'science of man': that is, the application of the new scientific method to the study of the human mind and its products. First amongst the particular, observable phenomena produced by the mind is, of course, language. And here we can see, from a methodological point of view, the need for and keen interest in a new rhetorical theory.

---

[4] Broadie, *Thomas Reid on Logic, Rhetoric, and the Fine Arts: Papers on the Culture of the Mind*, University Park, PA: Penn State University Press, 2004, p. xxiv.

Rhetoric in the classical tradition was concerned primarily with persuasion, but it became a key method of inquiry in the new science of man. It was seen as a tool for analysing the faculties of the mind that are observed in the processes of knowing, or coming to a belief or understanding. The Scottish rhetors were equally concerned with the implications of this knowledge; that is, with the formation of taste, of civic and personal virtue, and the creation of the bonds of sympathy and mutual understanding that form the basis of civil society. Their rhetorical theory is closely tied to a concordant philosophy of language, of aesthetics and the fine arts, and also of political philosophy. Amongst the thinkers included in this volume, many are indeed better known for their work in these allied fields: Francis Hutcheson is primarily considered a moral philosopher; Lord Kames was a leading legal thinker and historian who later turned to aesthetic inquiry; Alexander Gerard is known for his work on taste and genius; Adam Smith is identified with economics and political theory; Thomas Reid is most notable as a philosopher of mind. Only George Campbell and Hugh Blair are identified as rhetoricians, although, like the others, their rhetorical theory was a practical extension of a polymathic range of interests. Two other Scottish thinkers relevant to rhetorical history must also be noted, though with explanation, however, one for his inclusion in this list of rhetoricians, and one for his exclusion. Alexander Bain, living and working as he did almost a full generation after the Enlightenment, is an essential thinker in understanding how Scottish rhetoric was transformed in the nineteenth century and beyond. While it owes a great debt to the Scottish philosophy in which he himself was educated, Bain's work on rhetoric and his rhetorical textbooks reflect what happened when much later, largely experimental work on cognition and psychology met with Common Sense philosophy of language. Most of what is today considered to be the legacy of Scottish rhetoric owes more to the pedagogical trends advanced by Alexander Bain than to the more philosophical works of earlier Scottish rhetoric. Bain's influential writings helped develop the empirical tendencies of faculty psychology into a more positivistic perspective on language use. The most striking exclusion from this volume is David

Hume. Hume's work on the philosophy of mind and understanding is ever present in the work of his Scottish contemporaries, but his only direct writing on rhetoric, 'On Eloquence', though ostensibly dealing with the rhetorical art of oratory, is contradictory and notoriously difficult to interpret as rhetorical theory, and not easily included within the more identifiable concerns of Scottish rhetoric. Still, the exclusion of Hume from this volume should not be understood as a judgment on his relevance to Scottish rhetoric, only that his writings on rhetoric are primarily of interest to a more specialized audience.[5]

Themes in Scottish Rhetoric

Several hallmarks of Scottish rhetoric need to be highlighted, so that the reader may critique and compare their development in the readings that follow. The list is neither exhaustive nor definitive, but six themes — the rhetor's necessary orientation to the good, rhetoric as a moral art, the exploration of taste, the foundations of literary criticism, rhetoric as a means of personal improvement, and advocacy of simple style — provide a good guide to the rich and innovative Scottish contribution to an ancient and complex discipline.

The first consistent theme found in Scottish rhetorical theory is that effective rhetoric is intimately connected to the rhetor's own orientation to the true and good. Persuasion, and the creation of what is moving and pleasing to properly formed taste, is possible only when it is generated by one whose own moral and intellectual tastes have in turn been properly formed. This follows Ciceronian rhetoric, along with Quintilian's teaching that rhetoric is the 'good man speaking well'. In addition, however, it reflects the new territory that rhetoric occupies in its relation to the scientific

---

[5] A word might be said here also of the exclusion of John Witherspoon and his contemporary Scots in America. While Witherspoon was born and educated in Scotland, and is thus a product of the Scottish rhetorical tradition, his own rhetorical writings were written in and for the American context. For this reason they are better regarded as founding documents of the American rhetorical tradition.

method and experiential knowing. Scientific thinking is also concerned with what is true, even if its observations and the general laws they generate are probable truths only. Rhetorical skill is thus tied to *a posteriori* inquiry—the audience judges not only by language and skilled argument, but by what they observe through their own experiences of the speaker. Effective language touches the 'chord, which when struck, the human heart is made to answer' (Blair, **Reading XVII**). This shared, universal faculty registers pleasure at what is true, consistent, virtuous, and laudable. Whether we are using rhetoric or listening to it, good rhetoric relies on all the faculties, internal and external, to judge the product.

The second, possibly most important, theme of Scottish rhetoric—the affirmation of rhetoric as a moral art—is closely tied to the first. Language is the first foundation of civic life, the establishment of basic contracts, conventions, and habits all of which profoundly shape social intercourse and the foundations of civility, and influence moral action and formation. Language use activates our internal sense and for this reason the Scottish philosophers were keenly interested in investigating both childhood formation and the anthropological evidence of language development. Our internal inclinations and habits, they argued, are formed by internal and external patterns of understanding and approbation. Language is the tool by which we learn to distinguish, discern, and evaluate. Scottish philosophy thus conceives of rhetoric as the interface between the new science of man and its moral, ethical, and aesthetic implications.

That is why close attention was paid to what are now the most widely identified features of Scottish rhetoric, namely 'taste' and the foundations of criticism. Because language operates by social convention, the formation of those conventions is of great importance to civic life. Thus, how one's taste is fashioned—whether or not it functions properly to discern what is good and beautiful and derive pleasure from it—is a prerequisite not only of personal moral life and character, but of public ethics and standards of civility. For George Campbell, correct usage of language is what is 'reputable, national and present', and it is collectively exercised taste that generates these criteria. Like the ancients, the Scottish rhetoricians viewed rhetoric, properly conceived and developed, as the first condition to liberty; civil discourse is the condition of political freedom. The exercise of polite and civil taste in language use was consequently of great concern, so that its development became increasingly important as the new rhetoric took deeper hold in education. In the excerpts that follow, different authors treat the concept of taste differently. Alexander Gerard's theory is concerned to outline mental and sensory association and its moral implications, while Kames straightforwardly gives examples and descriptions of good (and poor) taste. Blair's concept of taste is deeply philosophical, though his pedagogical legacy has given him the reputation of an arbiter of eighteenth-century tastes rather than an aesthetic philosopher of language. It was Adam Smith who delivered the stunning first public lectures on Rhetoric and Belles Lettres in Edinburgh in the late 1740s, but Hugh Blair who held the first academic chair with this title, and the development of the modern English literature department in which the study and critique of texts is a separate academic discipline has been dated to his appointment to it in 1762. 'Belles lettres' — the appreciation and criticism of texts for their aesthetic value — had already been developed to some degree by the French academy. Smith was on the vanguard of bringing this new trend to Scotland, having studied at Oxford, where he read extensively in rhetoric, literatures of several languages, and the French belles lettres. Classical rhetoric had been limited to argument and persuasion, but as it responded to the development of logic it became more than the linguistic 'dressing' for argument. It made artistic expression in language its territory, and expanded its attention to other kinds of texts. Rhetoric was no longer simply an art of persuasion that made appeals to logos, ethos, and pathos. It now was the art of creating, and criticizing, language in all its written and oral forms. If the advancement of taste may be considered the third theme, the expansion of rhetoric to all things now considered literary may be counted the fourth.

An impulse to improvement constitutes the fifth notable theme in Scottish rhetoric. Its development as a discipline for the cultivation of taste and criticism was clearly a response to the new philosophy of mind, and its effect on logic and scientific method. But it was the political and social environment of Scotland in the eighteenth century that pushed it from the academy to the cultural centre stage. Scotland's growing political and economic freedom, together with an already well-functioning educational system, facilitated widespread interest in self-improvement for the purposes of personal advancement and civic participation. National improvement was also part of the agenda, because the 1707 Act of Union with England had made the Scots intensely concerned with national and cultural identity and historicity. Rhetoric had a two-fold part to play in this desire for improvement. First, as the discipline of the cultivation of personal taste, it was an aid to personal growth in the polite and civic arts, which in turn was expected to cultivate moral sensitivity. Secondly was a more pragmatic concern with language use as social currency favoured it. Smith was chosen for his public lectures not only for his knowledge of rhetoric and belles lettres and his skill as a teacher, but also for the 'correctness' of his speech and pronunciation. His lectures were considered edifying for his mastery of 'proper' English as well as their content. Though somewhat at odds with the rising interest in Scots Gaelic and national literature, the desire for greater social currency in the English political and economic system led to the avoidance of Scotticisms, and this particular kind of rhetorical 'improvement' was one of the sources of rhetoric's popularity, while the sixth, the advocacy of simple and direct style, is immediately related to it. Rhetoric as it was practised from Cicero on had tended to emphasize specific arrangement and ornate, carefully crafted style, so much so that rhetoric itself had become synonymous with lavish use of figures, tropes, and flowery impenetrability.

In addition to meeting the needs of the altered political and economic circumstances of the eighteenth century, the new rhetoric promoted a plain and simple style in response to the changing religious attitudes. The need was for religious and civil leaders to preach and discourse effectively to wider and more diverse audiences. Those who taught rhetoric at the universities in Scotland knew that many of their students intended to enter the Church or the Law, and that the old style of rhetorical ornamentation was not suited to congregations and juries who no longer came from one social and educational stratum. Howell noted that the earlier rhetoric had followed a 'ceremonial pattern', which was:

> Found by successive generations to be perfectly suited to their tastes in a culture dominated by splendid rituals and by elaborate political pageantries of imperial, royal, and aristocratic rule. But the Reformation and the Counter Reformation on the one hand, and the rise of the parliamentary government, on the other, tended to expose the uselessness of a merely ceremonial rhetoric and to create a thirst for the religious and political discourses that in content would be fully relevant to the facts of the given situation and in form would be simple and easy to grasp.[6]

In no place would both of these factors be more strongly at play than in Scotland, and nowhere therefore was the plain style more universally regarded.

The Extracts

Most of the authors included here were contemporaries, and many were intimate friends or close acquaintances. Francis Hutcheson, who opens this selection, along with Henry Home, Lord Kames, Alexander Gerard, Thomas Reid, and to a lesser extent Adam Smith, have not traditionally been included among rhetoricians. Hutcheson and Reid are more typically read as philosophers and for their wide influence on the Scottish school. For both of these authors, I have selected texts from their philosophical works that demonstrate the bearing philosophy of mind and philosophy of language have in understanding the rhetorical theory that developed under their influence. Hutcheson especially was in many ways a radical thinker. He succeeded Gershom Carmichael at the University of Glasgow, and was later succeeded by Adam Smith and Thomas Reid. He is therefore of the generation immediately prior to the rest of the authors (with the exception of Alexander Bain), and was an important influence on the philosophical milieu in which they were all educated. In his *Inquiry into the Original of Our Ideas Of Beauty and Virtue* (1725), he offers the outline of a moral and

---

[6] Howell, p. 446.

ethical system that can respond effectively to the egoistical challenge presented by Thomas Hobbes and Bernard Mandeville. Hutcheson argues that we have, in addition to the external senses, internal senses, among which is a moral sense, a sense of beauty, and a natural sociability. It is within the internal senses that language arises. Arts, including speech and poetry, are apprehended through our internal moral sense, by which we are stirred to participate in, and judge, the passions conveyed via the apprehension of 'universal goodness, tenderness, humanity, generosity... and our relish in beauty, order, and harmony' or their opposites. 'Upon this moral sense', Hutcheson tells us, 'is founded the power of the orator (**Reading I**). The audience needs no knowledge of rhetoric to be moved by it, and thus the ethical burden falls upon the rhetor. Hutcheson's fullest treatment of language is from his *System of Moral Philosophy* (1755) in which he devotes a chapter to 'Our Duty in the Use of Speech'. In this essay (**Reading II**) Hutcheson describes the moral sense as directed outward; we are interested in the good of others, we derive pleasure from what is good not just for ourselves but for all. At the essay's outset he summarizes language in the moral economy: 'As the power of communicating to each other our sentiments, desires, and intentions is one of the greatest blessings of the human species, so appropriately joined with our social feelings and affections, nature has also implanted a moral feeling in our hearts to regulate this power' (**Reading II**). It is from this articulation of the ethical nature of speech, and therefore of learning effective speech, that we see Scottish philosophy making language the central human faculty that mediates between the individual (in his senses and capacities), and society. Hutcheson is often noted for the fact that he was one of the first professors to teach in English, and consciously used his own rhetorical powers to stir an affective response to his teaching. On many of Scottish rhetoric's later themes and hallmarks, then, Hutcheson may be seen as both precursor and initiator.

Reid takes up these concerns from the perspective of moral philosophy. In the first extract I have chosen for this volume, he explains the basis of the principles of 'common sense', those that may be taken for granted in a philosophy of the mind. To do this, he relies on language not only as a kind of metaphor, but as itself an object for the application of the inductive method. 'The operations of our minds are denoted, in all languages, by active transitive verbs, which from their construction in grammar require not only a person and agent but likewise an object of the operation' (**Reading X**). In the second selection from Reid's work, he considers the philosophical implications of saying that some of the powers of the mind are, by virtue of a 'real foundation in nature', 'social intellectual operations' (**Reading XI**). Language is the primary indicator of the nature and existence of these operations, as well the means of conducting them. In the third extract Reid relates rhetorical inquiry to semiotics, and explores rhetorical responsibility and the nature of contract in his discussion of 'artificial' signs (**Reading XII**). This distinction between those parts of language which are 'artificial' (exist by mutual agreement of signification), and those that are 'natural' (are inherently demonstrative of a communication), points to the close relationship that Reid perceives between the mind and the body. The philosophical grounding of much of the work of Scottish rhetoric is found within this conceptual framework—the reunion of the mind and body and the inherently social operation of reasoning and perception.

Alexander Gerard is best known for his work in educational reform and his writings on the defence and evidence for Christian doctrine. However, his works on taste and genius link the moral sense developed by Hutcheson and Reid with the rising discourse on the development of taste as a major component in the ethics of reading, writing, and speaking. His 'Essay on Taste' (1759) won a contest held by the Philosophical Club in Edinburgh, leading to publication and a wide audience. While Gerard is certainly not the sole influence on the treatment of taste in the rhetorical texts of Campbell and Blair, his articulation of the aesthetic of 'fitness' can surely be counted as an important connection between the ancients and the Scottish Enlightenment. 'Utility, or the fitness of things for answering their ends', is, for Gerard, the key to aesthetic practice, on two levels (**Reading VIII**). First, a work of aesthetic value is one in which invention is purposefully deployed in directing the 'choice, disposition, and embellishment of its parts'. Second, our ability to see fitness is a chief source of aesthetic pleasure, and therefore the first concern of criticism. Taste itself is a kind of sensation that supplies us with simple perceptions entirely distinguishable from all that we receive by external sense or reflection. Thus taste is not sensory, or a pure idea, rather, it exhibits a set of perceptions that result from direct perception. The fitness of associated perceptions to communicate their qualities rouses our sympathy, which 'enlivens' our ideas, converting them to passions and in turn affecting taste. The excerpt from his 'Essay on Taste' included here (**Reading IX**) describes the relation of taste and genius in specifically rhetorical terms. He incorporates into the eighteenth-century discussion on taste, genius, and imagination the classical link between invention and execution.

This concept of fitness is also developed by Lord Kames. Whereas Gerard is concerned with the epistemology of taste, and its implications for the moral and ethical, Kames's *Elements of Criticism* is concerned with its practical development. Kames's position within the rhetorical tradition has been contested, and his *Elements* have rarely been read as rhetorical theory.[7] Yet the extract included here on 'Language of Passion' clearly conveys Kames's sense of eloquence and rhetoric as a fine art that can, and should, be criticized using faculties of judgment aligned both to universal standards of truth and to the properly functioning faculties of mind and emotion. Through copious literary illustrations, he gives examples of how to judge rhetorical usage for its fitness. A man of law by education and practice, Kames exhibits the impulse to teach the art of rhetorical criticism—how to judge. For example, he describes, 'words, being intimately connected with the idea they represent, the greatest harmony is required between them. To express, for

---

[7] For a discussion of this, and ways of reading Kames's *Elements of Criticism* as a rhetoric of criticism, see Beth Innocenti Manolescu, 'Traditions of Rhetoric, Criticism, and Argument in Kames's "Elements of Criticism"', *Rhetoric Review*, Vol. 22, No. 3 (2003), pp. 225–242.

example, a humble sentiment in high sounding words is disagreeable by a discordant mixture of feelings' (**Reading III**). Kames is as much concerned with rhetorical practice (the judgment of works and art) as with philosophical theory (the principles of human nature that produce his principles of criticism). His particular account of criticism embodies many of the themes that are later developed by Hugh Blair, as well as constituting the clearest example of the type of positivist criticism later generations would roundly challenge.

It was Kames who commissioned the young Adam Smith to give public lectures upon the subject of Rhetoric and Belles Lettres to the student body of Edinburgh, lectures he later gave to his students in Glasgow. Until the late 1950s, Smith's interest in rhetoric and literature was known, but nothing about its content. However, in the late 1950s, a set of student notes from his lectures in the academic year 1762–63 were found in an Aberdeenshire manor house by a John Maule Lothian, who transcribed and published them in 1963. While these lecture notes obviously cannot be taken as a wholly accurate account of Smith's thinking on rhetoric and belles lettres, they do give us enough intelligence to place Smith firmly at the vanguard of Scottish innovations in rhetorical theory. The selections included here offer insight into the many new directions in which Smith led his students' rhetorical understanding and usage. In them, the reader can see Smith's anthropological approach to language development, the subsequent national and regional emphasis on best use (see **Reading IV**), and his idea that proper style is not one absolute ideal which conforms perfectly to truth or beauty, but rather is that which is most fitted equally to rhetorical exigency and the character of the author (**Reading V**). In this respect, Smith's rhetorical theory is consonant with his ethical emphasis on the particular and practical as opposed to the general and speculative, which is also intimately tied to his ideas about sympathy and sentiment.[8]

---

[8] From *Theory of Moral Sentiments*: 'When we consider virtue or vice in an abstract and general manner, the qualities by which they excite these several sentiments seem in a great measure to disappear, and the sentiments themselves become less obvious' (IV, 2.2).

Reading VI provides some of Smith's most critical statements of the speculative bent to practical arts, and it is clear that he sees the practice of rhetoric as formative as well as indicative of character. Finally, in **Reading VII**, Smith ties his criticism of classical works and his theory of fittingness to both character and circumstance. He employs as the basis of his critical art an idea of historical, political, and economical contextualization that is radical both in its implications for the concept of rhetorical fittingness and because of its farsighted vision of the nature of criticism.

George Campbell and Hugh Blair are the only writers in this volume whose reputations rest primarily on their contributions to eighteenth-century rhetorical theory, so that their work has become the standard exemplar of Scottish rhetoric. This is not entirely inaccurate. George Campbell's *Philosophy of Rhetoric* was written over the course of several decades (begun in the 1750s and published in 1776), during which he presented parts of it as papers to the Philosophical Society in Aberdeen. In the process he had much time to think about its content with his friends and colleagues, including Thomas Reid, Alexander Gerard, and John Stewart, John Beattie, and Hugh Blair.[9] Campbell's *Philosophy of Rhetoric* is a discerning and thorough distillation of Common Sense epistemology, Humean philosophy of mind, and Baconian method, as well as classical and contemporary rhetorical theory. Some have speculated that its completeness may be one of the reasons why none of his contemporaries (notably Smith) wrote a philosophy of rhetoric.[10] Three of the most important chapters from Campbell's *Rhetoric* are excerpted here—his own 'Introduction', in which he lays out his rhetorical system (**Reading XIII**); Chapter 1, 'The Nature and Foundations of Eloquence', in which he describes the faculties to which eloquence (a word here nearly interchangeable for 'rhetoric') applies (**Reading XIV**); and Chapter 4, 'Of the Relation which Eloquence bears to Logic and Grammar', which makes a careful argument about the relation of truth to persuasion,

---

[9] Blair was not a member of the Aberdeen Theological or Philosophical Societies, but he was a personal friend.
[10] Howell, p. 579.

expanding the role of rhetoric from persuasion to consideration of 'not only... the subject, but also the speaker and hearers, and both the subject and the speaker for the sake of the hearers, or rather for the sake of the effect intended to be produced in them' (**Reading XV**). Blair explicitly takes up the social implications of this philosophical rhetoric in the 'Introduction' (**Reading XVI**) to his *Lectures on Rhetoric and Belles Lettres*. His opening paragraph declares that the improvement of thought, human reasoning 'is not the effort or ability of one, so much as it is the result of the reason of many, arising from lights mutually communicated, in consequence of discourse and writing'. More than merely staking out the rhetorical arts as a primary human, intellectual, and moral concern, he makes rhetoric and the cultivation of critical faculties for the development and judgment of language the key academic discipline. Blair's assertion that clear speaking and writing produces clear *thinking* is one that has been largely ignored as an Enlightenment idea — and it remains one still hotly discussed in composition pedagogy. I have chosen his chapter on 'Taste' so that readers may see the continuity and differences of Blair's rather practical explanation of it *versus* the more conceptual discussions in the previous selections. Blair's shadow loomed large on the teaching of rhetoric in the era that followed his own, and it is an interesting question of pedagogy whether or not later interpreters and teachers of rhetoric emphasized the theoretical, productive, or interpretive rhetorical actions outlined in Blair's lengthy textbook.

One of the factors affecting later interpretations of rhetoric was the nineteenth-century movement towards the empirical study of cognition and learning. The 'science of man' of the Scottish Enlightenment thinkers shifted from the 'science' of a proper epistemology, and philosophically-oriented psychology, to empirical, and often experimental, scientific inquiry into the physical workings of the mind and the emotions. At the forefront of this inquiry was Alexander Bain, founder of the journal *Mind* and an extremely influential academic educator and educational theorist. Bain's body of work is large, but for the purposes of demonstrating the pedagogical implications of the direction his work gave to Scottish rhetoric I have chosen a selection of one of his rhetorical textbooks.

Conclusion: Contemporary Relevance

As noted by Ferriera-Buckley at the outset of this introduction, rhetoric is a slippery term. It must, by its nature, encompass theoretical inquiry, but this is always in tension with its equally natural orientation to practice. To give the contemporary reader a proper understanding of Scottish rhetoric in its eighteenth-century development and articulation, and of its inestimably important influence on both the American university and the twentieth-century evolution of academic disciplines in the humanities, the rhetorical theory must be read alongside the pedagogical practices it inspired. The Scottish philosophy of rhetoric is part of the larger philosophical tradition, and it must be acknowledged that the two bodies of work — the philosophies and the rhetorics — are not synonymous. Nor are the texts synonymous with their interpretations and uses, especially as they were taken up in university instruction overseas. The attention that the present writers give to the philosophical and moral importance of what is circumstantial and specific must be seen in critical juxtaposition to the kind of rhetorical improvement with which Scottish rhetoric is most often credited in modern histories (the speaking of polite and proper English, free of possibly misleading regionalisms). Blair's textbooks (which 'went through sixty-two editions, fifty-one abridgments and ten translations in the century after its publication'),[11] and the legacy of Scottish rhetoric in general, has become in many ways coterminous with the self-improving impulse to use standard English on the part of Scottish and American students. James Berlin argues that when Blair's belles lettres tradition matured in American universities, uniting its attention to taste and literacy with the scientific approach to persuasion and human faculties, it proved the ideal discipline for the 'creation of the professional meritocracy consisting of an emerging middle class in the newly-elective

---

[11] Bizzell and Hertzberg, p. 657.

nineteenth century American universities'.[12] Following him, the American Compositionists of this century have made it a point to note in their own histories of rhetoric and composition that 'the source of current-traditional rhetoric[13] is to be found in Campbell, Blair, and Whately'.[14] This thesis has been readily accepted because of the widespread influence of Scottish Common Sense Realism in America at the time, which, it is assumed, provided appropriate grounds for positivist writing practices. However, this simple picture is complicated by the epistemological preference for local and specific language and its social and ethical ramifications as inductive evidence, the movement from classical languages to English vernacular that the Scottish rhetoricians promoted, and new works written in the Scottish dialects that they sponsored.[15]

These are just a few of the dimensions that a new inquiry into Scottish philosophy and rhetoric in its eighteenth-century context might profitably explore. This would offer an enhanced historical understanding, as well as providing a novel way of approaching many of the current debates on the practice and politics of language use. The selections offered here uncover many rhetorical issues that are not only still relevant to today's academic and political climate, but still very much alive in discussion, scholarship, and query.

---

[12] Berlin, p. 8.
[13] Current-traditional pedagogy is the turn from rhetorical instruction to 'composition' instruction. It teaches writing from the standpoint of an ideal final product: the essay composed strictly to answer its ends, with close attention to spelling and grammar. Current-traditional pedagogies teach a definitive 'right' writing final product, which is perfectly attuned to the needs of the audience (as explained in terms of cognitive or psychological science).
[14] Ibid.
[15] Blair personally sponsored the works of James McPherson and Robert Burns among others.

Works Cited

Aristotle, *On Rhetoric*, translated by George Kennedy, Oxford: Oxford University Press, 1991.

Berlin, James, *Rhetoric and Reality: Writing Instruction in American Colleges, 1900–1985,* Carbondale: Southern Illinois University Press, 1987.

Bizzell, Patricia and Bruce Hertzberg, *The Rhetorical Tradition,* New York: Bedford, 1990.

Broadie, Alexander, *Thomas Reid on Logic, Rhetoric, and the Fine Arts: Papers on the Culture of the Mind,* University Park, PA: Penn State University Press, 2004.

Ferriera-Buckley, Linda, 'The Eighteenth Century', in *The Present State of Scholarship in the History of Rhetoric,* Columbia: University of Missouri Press, 2010.

Howell, Wilbur Samuel, *Eighteenth-Century British Logic and Rhetoric,* Princeton: Princeton University Press, 1971.

Lothian, John Maule, 'Introduction' to *Lectures on Rhetoric and Belles Lettres, Delivered in the University of Glasgow by Adam Smith, Reported by a Student in 1762–63,* Edinburgh: Thomas Nelson and Sons Ltd., 1963.

Further Reading

Agnew, Lois, 'The Civic Function of Taste: A Re-assessment of Hugh Blair's Rhetorical Theory', *Rhetoric Society Quarterly,* Vol. 28, No. 2 (1998), pp. 25–36.

—, *Outward, Visible Propriety: Stoic Philosophy and Eighteenth-Century British Rhetorics,* Columbia: University of South Carolina Press, 2007.

Angus, Ian H., and Lenore Langsdorf, *The Critical Turn: Rhetoric and Philosophy in Postmodern Discourse,* Carbondale: Southern Illinois University Press, 1993.

Booth, Sherry, 'A Moment for Reform: Rhetoric and Literature at the University of Glasgow, 1862–1877', *Rhetoric Review,* 22.4 (Oct 2003), pp. 374–395.

Broadie, Alexander, *A History of the Scottish Philosophy,* Edinburgh: Edinburgh University Press (2009).

—, *The Scottish Enlightenment: Historical Age of the Historical Nation,* Cambridge: Cambridge University Press, 2007.

Craig, Cairns, *Intending Scotland: Explorations in Scottish Culture Since the Enlightenment,* Edinburgh: Edinburgh University Press, 2009.

—, *The Modern Scottish Novel: Narrative and the National Imagination,* Edinburgh: Edinburgh University Press, 1998.

Conley, Thomas, *Rhetoric in the European Tradition,* Chicago: University of Chicago Press, 1990.

Court, Franklin, *Institutionalizing English Literature: The Culture and Politics of Literary Study, 1750–1990*, Stanford: Stanford University Press, 1992.

Crawford, Robert, *Devolving English Literature*, Oxford: Clarendon Press, 1992.

Dickie, George, *The Century of Taste*, Oxford: Oxford University Press, 2003.

Gaillett, Lynee Lewis, ed., *Scottish Rhetoric and Its Influences*, Mahwah, NJ: Hermagoras/Erlbaum, 1998.

Golden, James L., and Edward P.J. Corbett, *The Rhetoric of Blair, Campbell, and Whately*, Carbondale: Southern Illinois University Press, 1990.

Hanley, Ryan Patrick, *Adam Smith and the Character of Virtue*, Cambridge: Cambridge University Press, 2009.

Horner, Winifred Bryan, *Nineteenth-Century Rhetoric: The American Connection*, Carbondale: Southern Illinois University Press, 1993.

Kennedy, George A., *Classical Rhetoric and its Christian and Secular Tradition, from Ancient to Modern Times*, Chapel Hill: University of North Carolina Press, 1999.

King, Edward, 'From Logic to Rhetoric', *Journal of Scottish Philosophy*, 2.1 (2004), pp. 48–68.

Lehman, William, *Henry Home, Lord Kames, and the Scottish Enlightenment*, The Hague: Martin Nijhoff, 1971.

Longaker, Mark Garret, 'The Political Economy of Rhetorical Style: Hugh Blair's Response to the Civic-Commercial Dilemma', *Quarterly Journal of Speech*, 94.2 (May 2008), pp. 179–199.

MacDonald, A.A., 'The Sense of Place in Early Scottish Verse: Rhetoric and Reality', *English Studies*, 72.1 (February 1991), pp. 12–27.

MacDonald, Alistair, and Kees Dekker, eds., *Rhetoric, Royalty and Reality: Essays in the Literary Culture of Medieval and Early Modern Scotland*, Medievalia Groningana N.S.7, Leuven, Paris and Dudley, MA: Peeters, 2005.

Manolescu, Beth Innocenti, 'George Mackenzie on Scottish Rhetoric', *Rhetorica*, (Summer 2002), pp. 203–275.

—, 'Kames's Legal Career and Writings as Precedents for Elements of Criticism', *Rhetorica*, 23.3 (Summer 2005), pp. 239–259.

—, 'Traditions of Rhetoric, Criticism, and Argument in Kames' Elements of Criticism', *Rhetoric Review*, 22.3 (July 2003), pp. 225–244.

McKenna, Stephen J., *Adam Smith: The Rhetoric of Propriety*, Albany: State University of New York Press, 2006.

McIlvanney, Liam, 'Hugh Blair, Robert Burns, and the Invention of Scottish Literature', *Eighteenth Century Life*, Vol. 29, No. 6.

Moran, Micheal, ed., *Eighteenth Century British and American Rhetorics and Rhetoricians: Critical Studies and Sources*, Westport: Greenwood Press, 1994.
Potkay, Adam, *The Fate of Eloquence in the Age of Hume*, Ithaca: Cornell University Press, 1994.
Short, Brian, 'Figurative Language and the Scottish New Rhetoric', *Language Sciences*, 22.3 (2000), pp. 251–264.
Warnick, Barbara, *The Sixth Canon: Belletristic Rhetoric and Its French Antecedents*, Columbia: University of South Carolina Press, 1993.

The editor would like to express particular thanks to Nelson Thornes Publishers for their permission to use extracts from Adam Smith's 'Lectures on Rhetoric and Belles Lettres', transcribed by John Lothian, published by Thomas Nelson (1963), and also to the kind assistance of Professor Daniel Carpenter for translating the (often antiquated) Latin and Greek texts quoted by authors. All translations not specifically provided by the original authors are Prof. Carpenter's.

One

Francis Hutcheson (1694–1746)

Born on 8 August 1694, just south of Belfast in Drumalig, Saintfield Parish, Francis Hutcheson had the good fortune to enter the world during the first period of relative peace for many decades in either his native Ireland or his ancestral Scotland. Entering the University of Glasgow at age 16, Hutcheson completed his undergraduate and MA in 1716. Upon receiving his MA, he followed his father into the ministry, studying for two years to receive his licence to preach in the Presbyterian Church. Hutcheson accepted an offer to found a dissenting academy in Dublin, where he taught for the ten years following his return to Ireland in 1718. While teaching, he wrote and published *An Inquiry into the Original of our Ideas of Beauty and Virtue* (1725), which achieved a wide audience and was revised and reprinted in 1726, 1729, and 1738.

Hutcheson's continued philosophical study led him to write *An Essay on the Nature and Conduct of the Human Passions and Affections, With Illustrations upon the Moral Sense*, published in 1742. Based on the reputation of these works, he was offered the Chair of Moral Philosophy at the University of Glasgow in 1729 upon the death of the previous chair, Gershom Carmichael. During his time there he published two textbooks, *Philosophiae moralis institutio compendaria*, in 1742, and, the same year, *Metaphysicae synopsis*. Both were republished in 1744, along with *Phneumatologiam Complectens*. At the time of his death in 1746, Hutcheson was working on *A System of Moral Philosophy*, which was published posthumously by his son in 1755, as was a translation of the *Compend* (1747) and *Thoughts on Laughter and Remarks Upon the Fable of the Bees* (1750). Within his works the rejection of egoism as the basis for moral action, and his promulgation of a positive view of human nature provided a popular counterpoint to the prevailing intellectual and theological climate of the time.

Hutcheson's influence as teacher was profound, both for the content of his courses as well as for his delivery. He was one of the first to lecture in the vernacular (as opposed to academic Latin), and his personal teaching practices were reflective of his philosophical stances on the importance of emotion and sentiment in motivating learning and volition. His student Adam Smith referred to him as 'the never to be forgotten Dr. Hutcheson', and Hutcheson had mutually influential correspondence with David Hume. The two men shared a critique of rationalism, belief in empirical methods, and the centrality of sentiment and feeling in experiential reasoning. However, he strongly disagreed with Hume's sceptical conclusions, especially upon the nature of virtue, and Hutcheson successfully blocked his appointment to the Chair of Moral Philosophy at Edinburgh, to Hume's lasting disappointment.

Hutcheson is not typically included in rhetorical volumes, although he is consistently cited as an influence on the rhetorical theories of George Campbell and Hugh Blair, and there is no question of his influence on Adam Smith, a key innovator of Scottish rhetoric. Yet, however little Hutcheson is read as a rhetorician, theorized language use is an essential component of his moral economy. As the following excerpts demonstrate, rhetorical knowledge and force are central to one's ability to move the passions of another, and also in the ability to be moved by the beauties of speech and writing. The sentiments, conveyed by language, both in its content and its form, appeal to the moral sense, and as such contain the user's obligation of responsibility to their affective outcome. Hutcheson considered the 'culture of the heart as the end of all moral instruction'.¹ His attention to moving the sentiments, and the psychology of emotion, returns the study of language to that of the classical appeals to *pathos* and *ethos*. It is interesting to note Hutcheson's position with regard to the relationship of language and truth, as he firmly places himself in the tradition which considers that rhetorical power is intimately connected to the rhetor's own relationship to truth and virtue, or, at least, should be.

Sources:

'Francis Hutchseson', Dictionary of Ulster Biography (ulsterbiography.co.uk).

Mautner, Thomas, Introduction to Francis Hutcheson's *On Human Nature: 'Reflections on our Common Systems of Morality' and 'On the Social Nature of Man'*, Ed. Thomas Mautner, Cambridge: Cambridge University Press, 1993.

Moore, James, 'Francis Hutcheson (1694–1746)', *Oxford Dictionary of National Biography*, Eds. H.C.G. Matthew and Brian Harrison, Oxford: Oxford University Press, 2004. Online Edition, Ed. Lawrence Goldman, 2008.

READING I[2]

An Inquiry into the Original of Our Ideas of Beauty and Virtue

Section VI. Upon this moral sense is founded all the power of the orator.[3] The various figures of speech are the several

---

[1] 'Preface' to *System of Moral Philosophy*, p. xxxi.

[2] Hutcheson, Francis, *Inquiry into the Original of Our Ideas of Beauty and Virtue*, Treatise II: Concerning Moral Good and Evil, Sec VI–IX: 237–247, London: J. Darby of Bartholomew Close, 1725.

[3] The 'moral sense' referred in this opening sentence is the primary subject of *The Inquiry into Our Original Ideas of Beauty and Virtue*, which he defines in the 'Preface' thus: 'These determinations to be pleas'd with any forms or ideas which occur to our observation the author chooses to call *senses*; distinguishing them from the powers which commonly go by that name by calling our power of perceiving the beauty of regularity, order, harmony, an *internal sense*; and that determination to be pleas'd with the contemplation of those affections, actions, or characters of rational agents, which we call virtuous, by the name of *moral sense*' ('Preface', vi). Hutcheson argues

manners which a lively genius, warmed with passions suitable to the occasion, naturally runs into, only a little diversified by custom: and they only move the hearers by giving a lively representation of the passions of the speaker; which are communicated to the hearers, as we observed above of one passion, viz., pity.

Now, the passions which the orator attempts to raise are all founded on moral qualities. All the bold metaphors, or descriptions, all the artificial manners of expostulation, arguing, and addressing the audience, all the Appeals to Mankind, are but more lively methods of giving the audience a stronger impression of the moral utility of the person accused, or defended; of the action advised, or dissuaded: and all the antitheses, or witticisms; all the cadences of sonorous periods, whatever inferior kind of beauty they may have separately, are of no consequence to persuade, if we neglect moving the passions by some species of morality. They may perhaps raise a little admiration of the speaker among those who already favour his party, but they oftener raise contempt in his adversaries. But when you display the beneficence of any action, the good effect it shall have on the public in promoting the welfare of the innocent, and relieving the unjustly distressed; if you prove your allegations, you make every mortal approve the undertaking it. When any person is to be recommended, display his humanity, generosity, study of the public good, and capacity to promote it, his contempt of dangers, and private pleasures; and you are sure to procure him love and esteem. If at the same time you show his distress, or the injuries he has suffered, you raise pity, and every tender affection.

On the contrary, represent the barbarity, or cruelty of any action, the misery it shall procure to the kind, the faithful, the generous, or only to the innocent and you raise an abhorrence of it in the breath of the audience, though they were not the persons who would have suffered by it. The same way, would you make a person infamous, and despised and hated, represent him as cruel, inhuman, or treacherous

---

that our faculties operate in such a way as to derive pleasure from all of these senses.

toward the most distant rational agents; or show him only to be selfish, given to solitary luxury without regard to any friend, or the interest of others and you have gained your point as soon as you prove what you allege. Nay, how far does it go to stop our admiration of any celebrated action to suggest, 'That the author of it was no fool,' he knew it would turn to his own 'advantage'.

Now, are the learned and polite the only persons who are moved by such speeches? Must men know the schemes of the moralists and politicians, or the Art of Rhetoric, to be capable of being persuaded? Must they be nicely conversant in all the methods of promoting self-interest? Nay, do we not see on the contrary, the rude undisciplined multitude most affected? Where had oratory so much power as in popular States, and that too before the perfection of the sciences? Reflection, and study, may raise in men a suspicion of design, and caution of assent, when they have some knowledge of the various Topics of Argument, and find them employed upon themselves: but rude Nature is still open to every moral impression, and carried furiously along without caution, or suspense. It was not the groves of the Academy, or the polished stones of the portico, or the managed horses of Greece, which listened to the Harp of an Amphion, or an Orpheus; but the trees, and rocks, and tigers of the forest: which may shew us, 'That there is some sense of morality antecedent to instruction, or metaphysical arguments proving the private interest of the person who is persuaded, to be connected with the public good.'[4]

Section VII. We shall find the same moral sense to be the foundation of the chief pleasures of poetry. We hinted, in the former Treatise, at the foundation of delight in the numbers, measures, metaphors, similitudes. But as the contemplation of moral objects, either of vice or virtue, affects us more strongly, and moves our passions in a quite different and more powerful manner than natural beauty, or (what we commonly call) deformity; so the most moving beauties bear a relation to our moral sense, and aired us more vehemently

---

[4] Hutcheson's footnote: See Treatise I. Sec. 2, Art. XIII, Sec. 4, Art. III.

than the representation of natural objects in the liveliest descriptions. Dramatic, and epic poetry are entirely addressed to this sense, and raise our passions by the fortunes of characters, distinctly represented as morally good, or evil; as might be seen more fully, were we to consider the passions separately. Where we are studying to raise any desire, or admiration of an object really beautiful, we are not content with a bare narration, but endeavour, if we can, to present the object itself, or the most lively image of it. And hence it is that the epic poem, or tragedy, give a vastly greater pleasure than the writings of philosophers, though both aim at recommending virtue. The representing the actions themselves, if the representation be judicious, natural, and lively, will make us admire the good, and detest the vicious, the inhuman, the treacherous, and cruel, by means of our moral sense, without any reflections of the poet to guide our sentiments. It is for this reason that Horace has justly made knowledge in morals so necessary to a good poet:

Scribendi recte sapere est & principium & fons.[5]

And again:

Qui didicit Patriae quid debeat, & quid amicis,
Quo sit amore Parens, quo Frater amandus, & Hospes,
Quod sit Conscripti, quo judicis officium, quae
Partes in bellum missi Ducis; ille profecto
Reddere Personae scit convenientia cuique.[6]

Upon this same sense is founded the power of that great beauty in poetry, the Prosopopoeia, by which every affection is made a person; every natural event, cause, object, is anim-

---

[5] Hutcheson ascribes this to *De Arte Poetica* V, verse 309. It may be translated: 'The source and font of writing well is to be wise.'
[6] *De Arte Poetica* V, 312:
 'He who has learned what he owes to his country and what to his friends,
 He who has learned by what love a Parent, a Brother, and a Guest must be loved,
 What are the duty of a senator, of a judge, what
 Are the roles of a General sent into war; that man truly
 Knows how to describe each person harmoniously.'

ated by moral epithets: for we join the contemplation of moral circumstances and qualities along with natural objects, to increase the beauty or deformity, and affect the hearer in a more lively manner with the affections described, by representing them as persons. Thus a shady wood must have its solemn venerable genius, and proper rural gods; every clear fountain, its sacred chaste nymph; and river, its bountiful god, with his urn, and perhaps a cornucopia diffusing plenty and fruitfulness along his banks. The daylight is holy, benign, and powerful to banish the pernicious spirits of the night. The morning is a kind, officious goddess, tripping over the dewy mountains, and ushering in light to gods and men. War is an impetuous, cruel, undistinguishing monster, whom no virtue, no circumstance of compassion, can move from his bloody purposes. The steel is unrelenting; the arrow and spear are impatient to destroy, and carry death on their points. Our modern engines of war are also frightful personages, with their rude throats counterfeiting the thunder of Jove. The moral imagery of death is every where known, viz. his insensibility to pity, his inflexibility, and universal impartial empire. Fortune is inimitably drawn by Horace with all her retinue and votaries, and with her rigid severe minister, necessity. The qualities of mind, too, become persons: love becomes a Venus, or a Cupid; courage, or conduct, a Mars, or a Pallas, protecting and assisting the hero; before them march terror and dread, flight and pursuit, shouts, and amazement. Nay, the most sacred poets are often led into this imagery, and represent justice's judgment as supporting the Almighty's throne, and mercy and truth going before his face: They show us peace as springing up from the earth, and mercy looking down from heaven. Everyone perceives a greater beauty in this manner of representation, this imagery, this conjunction of moral ideas, than in the fullest narration, or the most lively natural description. When one reads the fourth book of Homer, and is prepared, from the Council of the Gods, to imagine the bloody sequel, and amidst the most beautiful description which ever was imagined of shooting an Arrow meets with its moral epithet, 'The source of blackest woes', he will find himself more moved by this circumstance than by all the profusion of natural description which man could imagine.

History derives its chief excellence from the representing the manners and characters; the contemplation of which in nature being very affecting, they must necessarily give pleasure when well related. It is well known too, that a collection of the belt pieces of face-painting is but a poor entertainment, when compared with those pieces which represent moral actions, passions, and characters.

Section VIII. We are often told, 'That there is no need of supporting such a sense of morality given to men, since reflection, and instruction would recommend the same actions from arguments of self-interest, and engage us, from the acknowledged principle of self-love, to the practice of them, without this unintelligible determination to benevolence, or the occult quality of a moral sense.'

It is perhaps true, that reflection and reason might lead us to approve the same actions as advantageous. But would not the same reflection and reason likewise generally recommend the same meats to us which our taste represents as pleasant? And shall we thence conclude that we have no sense of tasting? Or that such a sense is useless? No: the use is plain in both cases. Notwithstanding the mighty reason we boast of above other Animals, its processes are too slow, too full of doubt and hesitation, to serve us in every exigency, either for our own preservation, without the external senses, or to direct our actions for the good of the whole, without this moral sense. Nor could we be so strongly determined at all times to what were most conducive to either of these ends, without these expeditious monitors, and importunate solicitors; nor so nobly rewarded when we act vigorously in pursuit of these ends, by the calm dull reflections of self-interest, as by those delightful sensations.

This natural determination to approve and admire, or hate and dislike actions, is no doubt an occult quality. But is it any way more mysterious that the idea of an action should raise esteem, or contempt, than that the motion, or tearing of flesh should give pleasure, or pain; or the act of volition should move flesh and bones? In the latter case we have got the brain, and elastic fibres, and animal spirits, and elastic fluids, like the Indian's elephant, and tortoise, to bear the burden of the difficulty: but go one step further, and you find the whole as difficult as at first, and equally a mystery with this determination to love and approve or hate and despise actions and agents without any views of interest, as they appear benevolent, or the contrary.

When they offer it as a presumption that there can be no such sense antecedent to all prospect of interest, 'That these actions for the most part are really advantageous, one way or other, to the actor, the approver, or mankind in general, by whole happiness our own state may be some way made better'; may we not ask, supporting the Deity intended to impress such a sense of something amiable in motions, (which is no impossible supposition) what sort of actions would a good God determine us to approve? Must we deny the possibility of such a determination, if it did not lead us to admire motions of no advantage to mankind, or to love agents for their being eminent triflers? If, then, the actions which a wise and good God must determine us to approve, if he give us any such sense at all, must be actions useful to the public. This advantage can never be a reason against the sense itself. After the same manner, we should deny all revelation which taught us good sense, humanity, justice, and a rational worship because reason and interest do confirm and recommend such principles and services; and should greedily embrace every contradiction, foppery, and pageantry, as a truly divine institution, without any thing humane, or useful to mankind.

Section IX. The writers upon opposite schemes, who deduce all ideas of good and evil from the private advantage of the actor, or from relation to a law and its sanctions either known from reason or revelation, are perpetually recurring to this moral sense which they deny, not only in calling the laws of the Deity just and good, and alleging justice and right in the Deity to govern us; but by using a set of words which import something different from what they will allow to be their only meaning. Obligation with them is nothing else but such a constitution either of nature, or some governing power, as makes it advantageous for the agent to act in a certain manner. Let this definition be substituted wherever we meet with the words, *ought, should, must*, in a moral sense, and many of their sentences would seem very strange. As that the Deity must act rationally — must not, or ought not to punish the innocent, must make the state of the virtuous better than that of the wicked, must observe promises—so substituting the definition of the words *must, ought, should,* would make these sentences either ridiculous, or very disputable.

READING II[7]

'Obligations in the Use of Speech'

I. We mentioned in the former chapter some natural principles which are plainly destined to regulate our speech. As the power of communicating to each other our sentiments, desires, and intentions is one of the great blessings of the human species, so appositely joined with our social feelings and affections; nature has also implanted a moral feeling in our hearts to regulate this power. We are naturally prone to communicate our sentiments. Truth is the natural production of the mind when it gets the capacity of communicating it, dissimulation and disguise are plainly artificial effects of design and reflection, and an immediate approbation naturally attends both this communicativeness, and the steadfast purpose of speaking according to our sentiments. In the exerting these powers of speech in the manner our heart at first approves, we must no doubt have a regard to some of the more general controlling principles in our constitution, so as not to follow any inferior one in opposition to the superior, as we must control sometimes and restrain the exercise of pity, gratitude, and other lovely principles when they interfere with the public happiness: but where candour, openness, and a sincere discovery of our sentiments does not interfere with it, the immediate feelings of our hearts suggest our duty and obligation to it, and that prior to the general obligation of using this powerful instrument of so many blessings in society in that manner which the general interest requires.

There are other ways in which we may communicate our sentiments, desires, or intentions, as by symbols, hiero-

---

[7] Hutcheson, Francis, *System of Moral Philosophy in Three Parts,* Glasgow: R. and A. Foulis, 1755. Vol. II, Chapter X, 'Obligations in the Use of Speech', pp. 28–43.

glyphics, painting, motions significant from nature, or custom. But speech and writing are by far the most distinct and useful signs.

II. To understand our duty in the use of signs, we must observe that grand[8] distinction among them, that some of them either by natural similitude and connection, or by custom, intimate to the observer a proposition, or give him occasion to infer it, without his imagining that the person who used these signs had any intention, or made any profession of communicating by them his sentiments or designs to him. Thus by seeing smoke, we conclude there is fire; by feeing it arise in many places of an hostile camp in an evening, we conclude that the army is not in motion; by feeing light all night in a window, we conclude that some person is watching; nor do we imagine that by these signs any person professes to communicate to us his sentiments, or to inform us of any proposition. But second, there is another use of signs, whether natural or customary, which plainly imports such a profession in the man who uses them; and 'tis only by doing so that they suggest to us any proposition.

This division of signs is different from that into *natural*, and *customary* or *instituted*. Both natural and customary signs may be so used as to import a profession of communicating our sentiments to others. The sending little wings or spurs to a friend at a distant court, signifies to him that he is in danger; and that only upon this justly presumed profession of ours to intimate to him our opinion about his danger. Designedly to deceive one by such signs, or by any hieroglyphics, would be as criminal as by a letter; and yet these are natural signs. On the other hand, instituted signs may lead one into a conclusion about our sentiments without his imagining that our using them was a profession of imparting our sentiments to him. A letter intercepted, or speech overheard by one to whom it was not addressed, may lead him to

---

[8] Hutcheson's footnote: A necessary distinction of signs. See Grotius, Hugo, *De Jure Belle ac Pacis* (1625), Book II, Ch. 21. & 8, no. ii. Also, Pufendorf, Samuel, *De Jure Naturae et Gentium Libri Octo* (1672). Book IV, Ch. 1.

such conclusions, while he yet knows there was no such intention or profession of communicating any thing to him.

III. As to signs importing no such profession, there is this general obligation in the use of them 'to do no determinant to any innocent person, or to the public, by leading men into any false conclusions which may be pernicious to them.' Wherever another has a right, perfect or imperfect, to know our sentiments, there even concealing them by silence, as well as all deception by any signs, is criminal. But where others have no such right, and much more where there is a just cause of war, so that even violence is lawful; or wherever deceiving others may do good; we may deceive them by such use of signs as imports no professions are justified by all, and may be used toward a friend for any innocent purpose. A studious man may darken his chamber that others may conclude that he is abroad.

But in that use of signs which imports a profession of imparting our sentiments, upon which their signification depends, the case is different. A great part of the pleasure of a social life arises from mutual confidence in each other's veracity in narrations, as well as promises. We often take our measures in dependence on the narrations of others, and derive from them much of our knowledge in human affairs. Deceiving others, therefore, designedly by signs justly understood as containing this profession of imparting our sentiments, and interpreted by them in the usual manner; as our hearts must immediately condemn the insincerity of it, so upon reflection we see it tends to deprive human life of all these advantages from mutual confidence in conversation.

This use of signs, too, imports a tacit convention to impart our sentiments to the person we address them to. Were not men persuaded of such an engagement, it would be vain and foolish to address speech seriously to another, or to listen to what is said. Suppose men imagined there was no obligation to veracity, and acted accordingly; speaking as often against their opinion as according to it; would not all pleasure of conversation be destroyed, and all confidence in narration? Men would only speak in bargaining, and in this too would soon lose all mutual confidence. Though we are not always obliged to disclose our sentiments, yet from these considerations it must appear that we are obliged, whenever we use signs in a way that imports a profession of imparting our sentiments, to be faithful in this profession; or to 'use them so as shall impart our real sentiments according to the reasonable interpretation of such signs.' And this is the general law of veracity.

IV. There are some necessary limitations of this rule, or some rules of interpretation of signs, especially of words, to be observed. First, when the signification of words, or other signs dependent on institution and custom, is changed from the old original one, we are not guilty of falsehood if their signification according to the present custom is true. Thus expressions of courtesy, and the ordinary designations of certain orders and offices, import no such opinions of the relations, or moral qualities of the persons they are addressed or applied to, as the words would import on some other occasions; and so nobody is deceived by them. They only signify our intention of common civilities, or of paying the ordinary deference to these stations.

Second, when in certain affairs 'tis known that men do not conceive it an injury to be deceived, there is no crime in false speech about such matters. This is the case in some diversions. In these trifling matters we see there is no mutual confidence, and thence may discern what would be the effect of falsehood in serious narrations. If in some few greater matters men have relinquished their claim to the veracity of others, there is no obligation to it. A tacit remission can free from a tacit convention; or rather in such matters, addressing speech to one imports no convention. No man censures a physician for deceiving a patient too much dejected, by expressing good hopes of him, or by denying that he gives him a proper medicine which he is foolishly prejudiced against: the patient afterwards will not reproach him for it. 'Tis true, men cannot be often deceived in such matters; confidence is soon lost in them. But that the good end may be obtained, the prejudice may be removed, and the patient does not disapprove the deceit. Wise men allow this liberty to the physician in whose skill and fidelity they trust. Or if they do not, there may be a just plea from necessity — of which more presently.

Third, nay, if false narrations are frequently practised on all sides in war; if the custom be so received that none complain of it as an improper artifice: however before the custom was received and known such narrations were unjust and treacherous; yet, when it is avowedly received, they can scarce be called unjust: since men seem mutually to remit their right. Such artifices indeed cannot be often repeated with success, as they are soon suspected.

The case is quite other ways in all serious narrations of men at peace. Nor indeed is the custom universally received in war. But as to any deceptions in any form of treaty or convention, even during a state of hostility, they never were or can be allowed as lawful. 'Tis by means of treaties alone that an end can be put to war without the cruel ruin and devaluation of one party; by treaties alone can any humane methods of war be received: to make them engines of deceit and hostility makes them useless, and all horrid devaluations must ensue: it must therefore be highly criminal.

Fourth, another limitation or exception allowed by most authors on this subject is when promises or narrations are extorted by the avowedly unjust violence of men who in their course of life renounce all the laws of nature: as 'tis alleged that they have forfeited all these rights of mankind, the maintaining of which to them would fortify or encourage them, or give them advantages in their wicked courses.

Fifth, another exception is obvious, when one has previously intimated to those concerned that he does not on a certain occasion speak according to his sentiments, or in the common acceptation of words. Thus when in teaching, men give examples of false propositions; or when men have declared that they appropriate certain ambiguous words to a signification different from what is common; or when friends have previously agreed upon meanings peculiar to themselves in their correspondence; there is no fault, though the words would intimate to others a false proposition.

Sixth, another exception, much insisted on, is in cases of singular imminent necessity, which 'tis alleged supersedes the obligation of many of the special laws of nature which bind us sacredly in all ordinary cases. As this plea from extraordinary cases of necessity is not peculiar to the subject of veracity in speech, we defer it to be considered more generally hereafter.⁹ And subjoin here some more special useful rules in which good men must agree.

IV. First, some special rules. The general advantages of sincerity and of the mutual confidence thence arising in society are so great, and the effects of insincerity and falsehood so pernicious, that if any exceptions are allowed in cases of necessity, the necessity must be very great and manifest, that it may over-balance the evils on the other side.

Second, wherever we are under obligation to impart our sentiments, we are bound to use such words as we judge most proper and effectual for that purpose; and to use other words designedly which we foresee will deceive the hearers, though in some other way of interpretation they may be true, is criminal. But in cases where we are not obliged to declare our sentiments, on account of the bad conduct or intentions of some hearers, or where our refusing to answer some captious questions might discover, as much as direct speech, what the inquirers have no right to know, and would abuse to the worst purposes, if they knew it; there it may be lawful to use such evasive answers, as a good unprejudiced mind, according to a just interpretation, would not intimate any thing false while yet we foresee that others will interpret the words another way, and be deceived by them, through their own temerity, or unjust prejudices. Of such speeches and answers there are instances in some of the most sacred characters.¹⁰

Third, a habit of sincerity so naturally attends and assists a virtuous disposition, and a contrary one is so pernicious, that all dissimulation and disguises, as well as direct falsehood, should be severely restrained in the young; nor ought they before the full use of reason to be allowed in such arts of concealment as a good man in mature years may sometimes justly use.

---

⁹ Hutcheson's footnote: See Ch. xvii of this book.
¹⁰ Hutcheson's footnote: Plato's *Republic*, 1, iii, seems to allow deception to be one of those powerful medicines which none but the skilful state-physician should use, and that too only on extraordinary occasions.

Fourth, there are some tenets of piety and virtue of such high dignity, and a good mind must have such an ardour to own and divulge them, that one is justified in openly declaring them at all hazards to himself, even when he has no prospects that others shall be brought into the same sentiments by these declarations. And wherever there is just ground of hope that such declarations shall do more good to the public by enlightening the minds of others, than what over-balances all our own sufferings we foresee, there we are obliged to such declarations and cannot innocently decline them: as when God has promised success by these means to a virtuous cause, or an institution most beneficial to mankind. And yet, on the other hand, where there is no rational hope of success, or of having any good influence on others, one cannot be said to be criminal in omitting such voluntary declarations as can no other effect than his own sufferings.

Fifth, as one most important end of civil power is the taking the decision of controversies, and the execution of justice, out of the hands of the interested and passionate parties, and committing it to unbiased men of wisdom interested on neither side; and to this all the subjects of a state have implicitly consented: 'tis the duty of a person cited as a witness in judgment, not only to maintain the strictest veracity in what he affirms, but to discover fully what he knows in the cause when required. And 'tis necessary in all states that severe punishments be inflicted on such witnesses as even conceal any thing required, out of pity, or favour to one whose cause they think just, or who has incurred the penalty of a law they may judge to be too severe. Were witnesses allowed with impunity to falsify, or to deny their knowledge of what they truly know, all civil judicatories would be useless: the decision of causes must remain in the hands of the imprudent, or such as are interested one way or another, as the witnesses generally are, by favour, or pity at least. If laws, or judges are too severe, or unjust, one would act the heroic part who rather than contribute to the sufferings of the innocent would refuse to give testimony, and submit to any penalty of refusing it, when thus he could obtain safety to the person in danger.

Sixth, as in addressing speech to others who have a right to know our sentiments, we do not merely profess that the words shall in some possible interpretation be true, but that they shall impart the truth in the ordinary acceptation in which a wise man would take them: since one might as well change all the significations of words, and make a new dictionary, according to which he might affirm or deny any thing, as make a new grammar, or way of construction unknown and unexpected by others. Both practices would destroy all use of speech: so, for the same reason, 'tis plainly unlawful to speak what in the terms expressed is false, though a secret reservation or addition would make the proposition true. No sentence is so false or absurd that it cannot, in this manner, be made true.

V. First, the former rules are designed to keep men from the crime of falsehood: but there are many others pointing out the duties, the virtues, and beauties of conversation, as speech may be the means of great good in human life. An honest heart possessed with kind affections to its fellows will incline to employ his conversation for their service as much as he can: such a one will desire useful knowledge in human affairs as a fund of good offices; his serious discourses will be instructive, or persuasive to something honourable, and even his gaiety will either be subservient to the same purposes, or at least innocent. And for these ends a winning courtesy in conversation, and even an agreeable external behaviour, is not unworthy of the regards of the highest characters.

Second, as all men have a tender sense of honour and reputation, and the utmost aversion to infamy, and the contempt of their fellows; as being esteemed and beloved by our neighbours is one of the sweetest enjoyments of this life, and suffering reproach, and infamy, and contempt, is among the bitterest afflictions to the finest spirits; all dispositions of humanity, all our moral notions of justice recommend to men the greatest caution about the characters of others. We may indeed look upon ourselves as at some liberty as to the measure in conferring praises or honours on men for any eminent virtues or services which happen to be ascribed to them. And yet even in this matter, a low, envious, poor spirit may be evidenced by denying the just praise to eminent merit, or by detracting from it, and studiously diminishing its importance. Such practices discourage all generous dispositions. Yet still each one is some way judge for himself as to the degree of eminent praises he will confer; and the right of others in this matter is only of the imperfect kind, though in men's judging as wrong, and violating such rights, they often discover a most odious disposition. But as to the simple character of integrity, honesty, and purity of manners, or the reputation of a good honest man, every one has a perfect right to it, unless he has forfeited it by grossly immoral actions. Unjust calumny and detraction, therefore, must be among the most grievous injuries; and the more odious that they can often be executed by hints, insinuations, shrugs, whispers in the dark.

Such as have any regard to virtue, to the goodness of their own hearts, or any moral worth, should the more carefully observe the first inclinations to such wickedness, and consider how base the roots are from which it springs. At best, from want of all examination at home, and a vain humour of talking about and intermeddling with other people's affairs; often from pride, and a mean delight in our own imagined superiority in virtue; often from a baser envy, when others are like to excel ourselves; and sometimes from an habitual sort of malice toward such as seem to vie with us in happiness, in wealth, in knowledge, or in popularity; or who have opposed any of our designs. Seldom are men led into such practices by any of the lovely dispositions of the heart even of a narrower kind; and all the generous and humane principles must make us abhor them.

Third, nay, suppose we are well assured of the secret faults or vices of others, it seldom can do good to divulge them. The restraint of shame, which is so powerful in life, is taken away when a character is lost. Public infamy may be too cruel a punishment to such as a private admonition might reform, who perhaps are already sincerely penitent, and repairing all wrongs as far as they can. Suppose a private admonition does not reform the offender, yet if the action can continue secret, and there be no fear of further injuries, or that others shall be seduced, 'tis hard to tell what is the advantage of publishing secret crimes. When there is hope that public censure may reform where private admonition prove ineffectual; where 'tis necessary to prevent future crimes, or the seduction of others; or to obtain reparation of damage, then it is prudent and just. But where these motives do not recommend it; where the secrecy can prevent the hurt of the example; where damages are repaired, and no new injuries apprehended; what can the divulging of faults do except gratify our ill-nature, or pride, or envy, or vanity in our superior purity, or an idle inclination to inconsiderate talking? The vicious are easiest reclaimed while the restraint of shame remains, which is loft by public infamy: the frequency of crimes makes them appear less shameful to others; their vicious inclinations are less restrained when they find that many indulge them, and the virtuous become more suspected of hypocrisy.

When indeed the gross vices of men are public, 'tis the duty of every society to declare their dislike of them; and yet to retain good-will toward the offenders, and endeavour to reclaim them. But while vice can be concealed, a good friend, or neighbour has the best opportunity of the kindest office to the offender, whom he may reclaim by admonition, and oblige in the highest manner, by concealing his faults.

Fourth, one of the most amiable and useful offices of life comes in on this subject: the reconciling friends, or neighbours who are at variance, by free conversation with both sides, representing the matters of offence in the most favourable lights, suggesting all extenuations, recalling past kindnesses, and presenting the great motives we all have to mutual forgiveness, since all of us need so often the mercy of God, and the indulgence of good men.

Fifth, under this head of the use of speech comes likewise in the old logical and moral debate between the Cynics and the other sects of ancient philosophy about obscenity. The Cynics allege that 'there is no work of God, no natural action, which may not be matter of inquiry and conversation to good men, and we must use their names'; hence, they conclude, 'there is no obscenity.' The answer to this is obvious.

Many words in every language, beside their primary signification of some object or action, carry along additional ideas of some affections in the speaker; other words of the same primary meaning may have the additional signification of contrary affections; and a third set of words may barely denote the object or action, without intimating any affection of the speaker. We shall find this difference in comparing the terms of contempt and indignation one uses when provoked, with those of the same primary meaning used by a calm man relating the same event. Few objects want these three sorts of names, one barely denoting it, another sort denoting also our joy or approbation, or our relish for it, and a third denoting our aversion or contempt of it. *Adultery, incest, fornication, lewdness,* denote these vices, and the dislike and condemnation of the speaker: other terms for the same actions may denote our liking them, and our lewd inclinations: a serious mournful account of any battle or unhappy riot has its grave words importing also pity and regret. A burlesque poem has its ludicrous words for the same things, importing our indifference and contempt of them. A chirurgeon[11] uses middle words, importing no passion of either kind.

An anatomist, or any modest man, can find words denoting any parts of the body, or any natural actions, or inclinations, without expressing any lewd dispositions, or any relish for vicious pleasures. In such words there is no obscenity. Other words may import an immoderate keenness for such pleasures, a dissoluteness of mind, a want of the natural modesty, a neglect of all the sober restrictions on our brutal appetites, and a recommendation of a dissolute conduct to others. These are the obscenities of conversation unworthy of a rational being, and opposite to the modesty of our nature; as well as all the manly principles of virtue.

In immoderate sensual enjoyments of other sorts there is vice; and a base despicable soul maybe discovered by great delicacy and concern about them. Conversation expressing such a low taste, or recommending it, may also be shamefully vicious. But as the amorous appetite is generally more violent, there is a sense of shame peculiarly fitted to restrain it; the breaking through this strong restraint of modesty, by our conversation, is generally more infectious and corrupting to others, who have not got a finer taste to make it wholly nauseous, than mean conversation about other sorts of sensuality.

---

[11] Archaism for 'surgeon'.

Two

Henry Homes, Lord Kames (1696–1782)

Henry Homes was born on his family estate in Berwickshire in 1696, where he was educated until the age of sixteen, when he was apprenticed to a lawyer in Edinburgh. His further study, however, was not in a university, but rather at the private law college of Prof. James Craig, and his own self-directed reading and attending of court sessions. Homes was raised to bar in 1724, and with the publication of *Remarkable Decisions in the Court of Sessions* (1728), and *Essays upon Several Subject in Law* (1732) he established himself as an important legal thinker of the day. During this period he became a leading figure in the Enlightenment culture of Edinburgh, both through personal friendships and active membership in intellectual societies. Kames' early tendency to self-educate revealed an extremely wide-ranging mind, an engaging and energetic personality, and, especially after his advantageous marriage (at what one early biographer called the 'prudent age of 47'[1]), the means and desire to support others' whose work he found valuable.

Kames' popular work, *Essays on the Subject of British Antiquities* (1745), begins his branching from legal inquiry to

---

[1] Chambers, Robert, *Biographical Dictionary of Eminent Scotmen*, 'Henry Home, Lord Kames', p. 275.

historical, and was written during his forced absence from Edinburgh during the Jacobite Risings of 1745 (for suspicion of Jacobite sympathies). Many years later, this work culminated in the pioneering volume of anthropology *Sketches on the History of Man* (1774). Homes was elevated to the bench in February of 1752, receiving at this time his family title of Lord Kames. He was appointed to the board of trustees for the Encouragement of Fisheries, Arts, and Manufacture in Scotland, which served to widen his influence and interests. During this time he also published *Historical Law Tracts* (1757) and *The Statute Law of Scotland, with Historical Notes* (1759); *Principles of Equity* (1760), concerning equity between the Scottish and English legal system, was followed by the *Art of Thinking* (1761). Lord Kames' move from legal philosophy to more general philosophy was fulfilled by his massive, three-volume *Elements of Criticism*, published only a year later, in 1762. Lord Kames had a deep interest in husbandry and gardening, and spent much of his time in his later years cultivating his estate, in addition to producing several other volumes on various subjects. He died on 27 December 1782, at eighty-seven years of age, having carefully said personal farewells to all of his friends and family.

It is hard to overestimate Kames' influence on the Scottish Enlightenment, including its development of Scottish rhetoric. His own *Elements of Criticism* was a standard teaching reference for style for many decades (it was reprinted 36 times), although his writing is notorious for not following his own rules of style. Perhaps as important as his own aesthetic figuring of the rules of rhetoric was his direct and immediate influence in the rhetorical innovation of others. It was Lord Kames who sponsored Adam Smith's first popular public *Lectures in Rhetoric and Belles Lettres* in Edinburgh. He was a close friend of Hugh Blair, who was in turn a close friend of Kames' cousin and friend, David Hume, and in contest and dialogue with these two he encouraged Blair to write his own lectures (Blair later became the first Regius Professor of Rhetoric and Belles Lettres at Edinburgh). Amongst his many areas of interest for improving Scottish society, Kames was keenly interested in the social implications of properly formed taste: 'A uniformity of taste and sentiment in matters of importance forms an intimate connection among individuals, and is a great blessing in the social state'.[2] It is for this reason he includes rhetorical instruction amongst his other projects for the improvement of Scottish society.

Sources

Chambers, Robert, *Biographical Dictionary of Eminent Scotmen*, Vol. 2, half-volume 4, pp. 272–276, 1875. National Library of Scotland Online Collections.

Durie, Alastair J. and Stuart Handley, 'Home, Henry, Lord Kames (1696–1782)', *Oxford Dictionary of National Biography,* Online Edition, Ed. Lawrence Goldman, Oxford: Oxford University Press, 2004.

Ross, Ian Simpson, *Lord Kames and the Scotland of His Day,* Oxford: Oxford University Press, 1972.

READING III[3]

'The Language of Passions'

Among the particulars that compose the social part of our nature, a propensity to communicate our opinions, our emotions, and everything that affects us, is remarkable. Bad fortune and injustice affect us greatly; and of these we are so prone to complain, that if we have no friend nor acquaintance to take part in our sufferings, we sometimes utter our complaints aloud, even where there is no one to listen.

But this propensity operates not in every state of mind. A man immoderately grieved, seeks to afflict himself, rejecting all consolation: immoderate grief accordingly is mute: complaining is struggling for consolation.

It is the wretch's comfort still to have
Some small reserve of near and inward woe,
Some unsuspected hoard of inward grief,
Which they unseen may wail, and weep, and mourn,
And glutton-like alone devour
—'Mourning Bride', Act 1, Sc. 1

---

[2] *Elements of Criticism*, 'The Standards of Taste'.
[3] Kames, Lord Henry Home, *Elements of Criticism,* Fourth Edition, Kincaid and Bell, 1769, Chapter XVII, pp. 312–320.

When grief subsides, it then and no sooner finds a tongue: we complain, because complaining is an effort to disburden the mind of its distress.

Surprise and terror are silent passions for a different reason: they agitate the mind so violently as for a time to suspend the exercise of its faculties, and among others the faculty of speech.

Love and revenge, when immoderate, are not more loquacious: moderate love, when unsuccessful, is vented in complaints; when successful is full of joy expressed by words and gestures.

As no passion has any long uninterrupted existence, nor does it beat always with one pulse. The language suggested by passion is not only unequal, but frequently interrupted: and even during uninterrupted fits of passion, we only express in words the more capital sentiments. In familiar conversation, one who vents every single thought is justly branded with the character of loquacity; because sensible people express no thoughts but what make some figure: in the same manner, we are only disposed to express the strongest pulses of passion, especially when it returns with impetuosity after interruption.

I formerly had occasion to observe, that the sentiments ought to be tuned to the passion, and the language to both. Elevated sentiments require elevated language: tender sentiments ought to be clothed in words which are soft and flowing. When the mind is depressed with any passion, the sentiments must be expressed in words that are humble, not low. Words, being intimately connected with the ideas they represent, so the greatest harmony is required between them. To express, for example, a humble sentiment in high sounding words, is disagreeable by a discordant mixture of feelings: and the discord is not less when elevated sentiments are dressed in low words:

Veribus exponi tragicis res comica non vult.
Indignatur item privatus ac prope focco
Dignis carminibus narrari coena Thyefae.[4]

---

[4] The modern text for this reads somewhat differently:

—Horace, *Ars poetica*, 1.89

This, however, excludes not figurative expression, which within moderate bounds communicates to the sentiment an agreeable elevation. We are sensible of an affect directly opposite where figurative expression is indulged beyond a just measure: the opposition between the expression and the sentiment makes the discord appear greater than it is in reality.

At the same time, figures are not equally the language of every passion: pleasant emotions, which elevate or swell the mind, vent themselves in strong epithets and figurative expression; but humbling and dispiriting passions affect to speak plain:

Et tragicus plerumque dolet fermone pedestri
Telephus et Pelcus: cum pauper et exul uterque
Projicit ampullus et sesquipedalian verba,
Si curat cor spectantis testigiffe querela.[5]
—Horace, *Ars poetica*, 1. 95

Figurative expression, being the work of an enlivened imagination, cannot be the language of anguish or distress. Otway, sensible of this, has painted a scene of distress in

---

> *Versibus exponi tragicis res comica non vult*
> *Indignatur item privates ac prope socco*
> *Dignis carminibus narrari cena Thyestae.*
> It may be translated: 'A comic theme does not want to be expounded with tragic verses; likewise, the Feast of Thyestes resents being told in common strains worthy of comic costume.' The *socco* (comic costume) is literally 'shoe', referring to the shoes worn for clowning (Prof. D. Carpenter).

[5] The modern text of this is somewhat different:
> *Et tragicus plerumque dolet sermone e pedestri*
> *Teleplus et Pelecus, cum pauper et exsul uterque*
> *Pricit ampullus et sesquipedalia verba*
> *Si curat cor spectantis tergisse querella.*
> It may be translated: 'And tragic Telephus and Peleus often grieve in pedestrian language (ie., prose)
> When as a pauper and an exile each
> Abandons bombast and words a foot and a half long,
> If he should care that his complaints touch the heart of the spectator' (Prof. D. Carpenter).

colours finely adapted to the subject: there is scarce a figure in it, except a short and natural simile with the speech introduced. Belvidera talking to her father of her husband:

Think you saw what past at our last parting;
Think you beheld him like a raging lion,
Pacing the earth, and tearing up his step,
Fate in his eyes, and roaring with the pain
Of buringin fury; think you saw his one hand
Fix'd on my throat, while the extended other
Grasp'd a keen threat'ning dagger; oh, 'twas thus
We last embrac'd, when trembling with revenge,
He dragged me to the ground, and at my bosom
Presented horrid death; cry'd out, My friends!
Where are my friends? Swore wept rag'd, threaten'd, lov'd;
For yet he lov'd, and that dear love preserv'd me
To this last rial of a fahter's pity.
I cannot fear death, but cannot bear a thought
That that dear hand should do th' unfriendly office:
If I was ever then your care, now hear me;
Fly to the Senate, save the promise'd lives
Of his dear friends, ere mine be made the sacrifice.
—'Venice Preserved', Act V.

To preserve the foresaid resemblance between words and their meaning, the sentiments of active and hurrying passions ought to be dressed in words where syllables prevail that are pronounced short or fast; for these make an impression of hurry and precipitation. Emotions, on the other hand, that rest upon their objects, are best expressed by words where syllables prevail that pronounced long or slow.

A person affected with melancholy has a languid and slow train of perceptions. The expression best suited to that state of mind is where words, not only of long, but of many syllables abound in the composition; and, for that reason, nothing can be finer than the following passage:

In those deep solitudes, and awful cells,
Where heavenly-pensive Contemplation dwells,
And ever-musing Melancholy reigns.
—Pope, *Eloise to Abelard* (lines 1–3)

To preserve the same resemblance, another circumstance is requisite, that the language, like the emotion, be rough or smooth, broken or uniform. Calm and sweet emotions are best expressed by words that glide softly: surprise, fear, and other turbulent passions, require an expression both rough and broken.

It cannot have escaped any diligent enquirer into nature that in the hurry of passion one generally expresses that thing first which is most at heart: which is beautifully done in the following passage:

Me, me: adsum qui seci: in me convertite ferrum
O Rutuli, mea sraus omnis.[6]
—*Aeneid*, ix. 427

Passion has often the effect of redoubling words, the better to make them express the strong conception of the mind. This is finely imitated in the following examples.

…Thou sun, said I, fair light!
And thou enlighten'd earth, so fresh and gay!
Ye hills and dales, ye rivers, woods, and plains!
And ye that live, and move, fair creature! Tell,
Tell is ye saw, how came I thus, how here…
—*Paradise Lost*, Book viii, 273

…Both have sinn'd! but thou
Against God only; I, 'gainst God and thee:
And to the place of judgment will return.
There with cries importune Heaven, that all
The sentence, from thy head remov'd, may light
On me, sole cause to thee of all this woe;
Me! Me! Only just object of his ire.
—*Paradise Lost*, Book x, 930

Shakespeare is superior to all other writers in delineating passion. It is difficult to say in what part he most excels,

---

[6] The modern text of this is somewhat different:
Me, me adsum qui feci: in me convertite ferrum
O Rutuli! Mea fraus omnis.
It may be translated: 'Me, me! I did it; turn you iron against me O Rutulians! It was my fault' (Prof. D. Carpenter).

whether in moulding every passion to peculiarity of character in discovering the sentiments that proceed from various tones of passions, or of expressing properly every different sentiment. He disgusts not his reader with general declamation and unmeaning words, too common with writers; his sentiments are adjusted to the peculiar character and circumstances of the speaker; and the propriety is no less perfect between his sentiments and his diction. That this is no exaggeration will be evident to every one of taste, upon comparing Shakespeare with other writers in similar passages. If upon any occasion he fall below himself, it is in those scenes where passion enters not: by endeavouring in that case to raise his dialogue above the style of ordinary conversation, he sometimes deviates into intricate thought and obscure expression: Sometimes, to throw his language out of the familiar, he employs rhyme. But may it not in some measure excuse Shakespeare, I shall not say his works, that he had no pattern, in his own or any living language, of dialogue fitted for the theatre? At the same time, it ought not to escape observation, that the stream clears in its progress that in his later plays he has attained the purity and perfection of dialogue; an observation that with great certainty than tradition, will direct us to arrange his plays in the order of time. This ought to be considered by those who rigidly exaggerate every blemish of the finest genius for drama ever the world enjoyed: they ought also for their own sake to consider, that it is easier to discover his blemishes, which lie generally at the surface, than his beauties, which cannot be truly relished but by those who dive deep into human nature. One thing must be evident to the meanest capacity, that wherever passion is to be displayed, Nature shows its might in him, and is conspicuous by the most delicate propriety of sentiment and expression.

I return to my subject from a digression I cannot repent of. That perfect harmony which ought to subsist among all the constituent parts of a dialogue, is a beauty, no less rare than conspicuous: as to expression in particular, where I to give instances, where, in one or other of the respects above mentioned, it corresponds not precisely to the characters, passions, and sentiments, I might from different authors collect volumes. Following therefore the method laid down in the chapter on sentiments, I shall confine my quotations to the grosser errors, which every writer ought to avoid.

And, first, of passions expressed in words flowing in an equal course without interruption.
[...]

If in general, the language of violent passion ought to be broken and interrupted, soliloquies ought to be so in a particular manner language in intended by nature for society; and a man when alone, though he always clothes his thoughts in words, seldom gives his words utterance, unless then prompted by some strong emotion; and even then by starts and intervals only. Shakespeare's soliloquies may be justly established as a model.
[...]

Then next class are the grosser errors which all writers ought to avoid shall be of language elevated above the tone of sentiment.
[...]

Language too artificial or too figurative for the gravity, dignity, or importance, of the occasion may be put in the third class... nothing can be contrived in language more averse to the tone of the passion than florid speech: I should imagine it apt more to provoke laughter than inspire concern or pity.

In the fourth class shall be specimens of language too light or airy for a severe passion... A thought that turns the expression instead of the subject, commonly called a *play of words*, being low and childish, is unworthy of any composition, whether gay or furious, that pretends to any degree of elevation: thoughts of this kind make a fifth class.
[...]

Antony speaking of Julius Caesar:
O world! Thou wast the sorest of this heart,
And this, indeed, O world, the heart of thee,
How like a deer, stricken by many princes,
Dost thou here thou lie!
—*Julius Caesar*, Act 3, Sc. 3

Playing thus with the sound of words, which is still worse than a pun, is the meanest of conceits. But Shakespeare when he defend to a play of words, is not always in the wrong; for it is done sometimes to denote a peculiar character... jingle of words is the lowest species of that low wit; which is scarce sufferable in any case, and least of all in a heroic poem: and yet Milton, in some instances has descended to that puerility:

And brought into the world a world of woe
—begirt th'Almighty throne
Beseeching or besieging—
Which tempted our attempt—
At one flight bound high overleape'd all bound,
—with a shout
loud as from numbers without number.[7]

One should think it unnecessary to enter a caveat against an expression that has no meaning, or no distinct meaning; and yet somewhat of that kind may be found even among good writers. Such make a sixth class.

---

[7] This does not appear to be from directly from Milton, rather from Joseph Addison's critique of Milton. See the *Spectator,* no. 297, p. 37.

Three
Adam Smith
(1723–1790)

Adam Smith, one of the most celebrated Scots of any century, was born in Kirkcaldy on 5 June 1723. His father had died six months before he was born, and his mother raised him on her own, with the help of influential relatives. After an early education at the parish school, Smith entered the University of Glasgow at age 14. Francis Hutcheson became one of his most influential teachers, and Smith took as many courses with him as he could. He became an accomplished student of natural and moral philosophy, winning upon graduation the prestigious Snell Exhibition to further his studies at Balliol College, Oxford. While in Oxford, Smith, unimpressed with the teaching he experienced, turned his attention to a self-directed usage of the libraries at his disposal, becoming deeply versed in rhetorical theory and history, the timely subject of belles lettres, deeper knowledge of Latin and Greek, and teaching himself French and Italian. Smith had been considering the ministry, but the anecdotal story goes that he gave it up upon receiving a harsh reprimand by his superior for being discovered reading Hume's *Treatise of Human Nature*.

Upon returning to Scotland in 1746, Smith spent two years at home with his mother before moving to Edinburgh to undertake the teaching of a public course in Rhetoric and Belles Lettres. Henry Home, Lord Kames, was the chief sponsor of these lectures, and they were very popular and well attended. Smith continued them for two years to an audience of primarily law and theology students from the University of Edinburgh, including Hugh Blair, James Oswald, John Millar, Alexander Wedderburn, and others. During this time, Smith also delivered his Lectures to one of the societies in Edinburgh (most likely the Philosophical Society). His reputation as a scholar of note being secured, Smith was offered the Chair of Logic and Rhetoric at the University of Glasgow in 1751. He served this for only a year, taking the Chair of Moral Philosophy in 1752, which give him the opportunity to create lectures on another of his subjects of interest, political philosophy and political economy. He first expanded his ethical theories into the *Theory of Moral Sentiments*, which was published in 1759. In 1764 Smith resigned his university post to become the private tutor to the young Duke of Buccleuch on his European tour. This post enabled Smith to meet and speak with Voltaire, and participate in his good friend David Hume's circles in Paris while he worked on his next venture, *The Wealth of Nations*. Upon the death of the Duke's younger brother in 1766, Smith returned from the Continent and spent some time on a revision of *Theory of Moral Sentiments*. He spent the next six years at his home on Kirkcaldy, and another three in London, working on *The Wealth of Nations*, which was finally published, to lasting acclaim, in 1776.

In his Lectures, he is the first of the Scottish rhetoricians to equate the mode of expression with the method of thinking it represents. Rhetoric as a 'science of the mind' would become a distinctive hallmark of Scottish Enlightenment rhetoric. Another important part of Smith's rhetorical legacy is the fact that, as a practitioner of language himself, he was noted for his pronunciation and delivery: it was of keen interest to Scots during this period to be able to speak in the coin of the realm, that is, to have the ability to adapt pronunciation to situations where native Scots inflection would be a disadvantage. Smith, it can be assumed partly because of his six years at Oxford, could model a more educated English style of speaking, and his personal style was widely admired. It was partly this desire for 'improvement' that drove the popularity of courses in rhetoric, although that is not at the heart of the philosophical and ethical project of the rhetorical innovation. Sadly, for scholars of Smith and of rhetoric, Smith had his manuscripts and papers burned by his solicitors before his death in Edinburgh on 17 June 1790. What papers he left were published in 1795 as *Essays on Philosophical Subjects*.

In his later years, Smith had returned to his earlier interests, and was working on a 'philosophical history of all the different branches of Literature, Philosophy, Poetry, and Eloquence', as well as a history of law. The following excerpts are from lecture notes from two unknown students of his course in Rhetoric and Belles Lettres in Glasgow in 1764. They are the only remaining writings on rhetoric by Smith himself, though indirectly, and even they were not found until unearthed at an estate sale in Aberdeenshire by Prof. John Lothian in 1958. The immense influence of Smith on the formation of political philosophy and economics has largely eclipsed his own profound thinking in rhetorical theory and practice, but it is hoped that recent attention to the roots and legacies of Scottish philosophy may bring new scholars to this important area of Smith's work.

Sources

Bryce, J.C., 'Introduction', his transcription of Smith's *Lectures on Rhetoric and Belles Lettres*, Glasgow Edition of the Works and Correspondence of Adam Smith, Oxford: Oxford University Press, 1983.

McKenna, Stephen, *Adam Smith: The Rhetoric of Propriety*, Albany, NY: State University of New York Press, 2006.

Winch, David, 'Smith, Adam (b. 1723, died 1790)', *Oxford Dictionary of National Biography*, Ed. H.C.G. Matthew and Brian Harrison, Oxford: Oxford University Press, 2004. Online Edition Ed. Lawrence Goldman, Oct. 2007.

Editorial note: The following excerpts are from John Maule Lothian's transcriptions from the student notes he found in 1958, and published in 1963 under T. Nelson and Sons, Publishers. Because these transcriptions are Prof. Lothian's copyrighted work, I have not taken editorial liberties, and maintained throughout his original markings and relevant footnotes. The following conventions are used: ( ) brackets originally in the manuscript; < > passages originally written on the verso pages of the manuscript, written in the same hand and ink as the main text; [ ] editorial brackets— emendations, or omissions supplied. In the footnotes, I have indicated which of them are Lothian's original, and which are mine.

READING IV[1]

Lecture 2, Friday, 19 November, 1762

Perspicuity requires not only that the expressions we use should be free from all ambiguity proceeding from synonymous words, but that the words should be natives (if I may <say> so) of the language we speak in. Foreigners, though they may signify the same thing, never convey the idea with such strength as those we are acquainted with and whose origin we can trace. We may see an instance of this in the word 'unfold'; a good old English word derived from an English root; and consequently its meaning must be easily perceived. This word, however has within these few years been most unaccountably thrust put of common use by a French word of not half the strength or significance, to wit, 'develop'. This though of the same signification with 'unfold' can never convey the idea so strongly to an English reader. <In the same manner 'unravel' is thrown out to make room for [blank]>.[2] The words of another language may, however, be naturalized by time and be as familiar to us as those which are originally our own, and may then be used with as great freedom. But here likewise we may see the effect of the words being well known to us or not. For instance, the words 'insufferable' and 'intolerable' which are both borrowed of the Latin language and compounded of words of the same meaning, are of very unequal strength. The reason is that the word 'intolerable' has not been so long introduced amongst us and therefore does not carry the same power along with it. We say that the cruelty and oppression of a tyrant is 'insufferable', but the heat of a summer's day is 'intolerable'.

---

[1] From Adam Smith's 'Lectures on Rhetoric and Belles Lettres', transcribed by John Lothian, published by Thomas Nelson (1963), pp. 1–6.

[2] The [blank] has been filled up by a later hand with the word 'develop'; this in turn has been cancelled and 'perhaps 'explicate'' substituted. (Lothian.)

'Insufferable' expresses our emotion and indignation at the behaviour of the tyrant, whereas 'intolerable' means only that there is some difficulty and uneasiness in supporting the heat of the sun.

The English language perhaps needs our care in this respect more than any other. New words are continually pushing out our own original ones, so that the stock of our own is now become but very small and is still diminishing. This perhaps is owing to a defect which our language labours much under, of being compounded of a great number of others. <No author has been more attentive to this point than Swift; we may say his language is more English than any other writer that we have.> Most terms of art and most compounded words are borrowed from other languages, so that the lower sort of people, and those who are not acquainted with those languages from whence they are taken, can hardly understand many of the words of their own tongue. Hence it is that we see this sort of people are continually using these words in meanings altogether foreign to their proper ones. The Greeks used compounded words, but then they were formed from words of their own language. By this means their language was so plain that the meanest person would perfectly understand the terms of art and expressions of any artist or philosopher. The word 'triangle' would not be understood by an Englishman who had not learned Latin, but an Italian would at the first understand their '*triangulo*' or a Dutchman their '*thrienuik*'.

Our words must not only be English and agreeable to the custom of the country, but likewise to the custom of some particular part of the nation. This part undoubtedly is formed of the men of rank and breeding. The easiness of those persons' behaviour is so agreeable and taking that whatever is connected with it pleases us. (It is commonly said also that in France and England the conversation of the ladies is the best standard of language, as there is a certain delicacy and agreeableness in their behaviour and address, and in general we find that whatever is agreeable makes what accompanies it have the deeper impression and convey the notion of agreeableness along with [it]. For this reason we love both their dress and their manner of language.)

On the other hand many words, as well as gestures or peculiarities of dress, give us an idea of some thing mean and low in those in whom we find them. Hence it is that words equally expressive and more commonly used would appear very absurd if used in common conversation by one in the character of a gentleman. Thus perhaps nine-tenths of the people of England say, 'Is'e do't' instead of 'I will do it', but no gentleman would use that expression without the imputation of vulgarity. We may indeed naturally expect that the better sort will often exceed the vulgar in the propriety of their language but where there is no such excellence we are apt to prefer those in use amongst them, by the association we form betwixt their words and the behaviour we admire in them. It is the custom of the people that forms what we call propriety, and the custom of the better sort from whence the rules of purity of style are to be drawn. As those of the higher rank generally frequent the court, the standard of our language is therefore to be met with there chiefly. In countries, therefore, which are divided into a number of sovereignties, we cannot expect to meet with any general standard, as the better sort are scattered into different places. Accordingly we find that in Greece and Modern Italy each State sticks by its own dialect, without yielding the preference to any other, even though superior in other respects, as the Athenians were.

Our words must also be put in such order that the meaning of the sentence shall be quite plain and not depend on the accuracy of the printer in placing the points or of the readers in laying the emphasis on any certain words. Mr. Pope often errs in both these respects: as, first, in that line, 'Born but to die, and reasoning but to err'.[3] The sense of this line is very different in these two cases, when we put the accent in both members on *but*, or in the one on *born* and in the other on *reasoning*. The former I imagine was Mr. Pope's own meaning, though Mr. Warburton gives it a different turn.[4] But if that had been Mr. Pope's meaning Mr. Pope had more prop-

---

[3] *Essay on Man*, II, l. 10. (Lothian.)
[4] Warton, (ed.), *Works of Pope*, III, 57, gives a note by Warburton on l.II not relevant to l.10. (Lothian.)

erly have used *though* for *but* and then there had been no ambiguity, though the line would not have been so strong as in the way it stands at present if taken in the common and apparent meaning. We have an example of the latter sort, when it is not easy to know what member of the sentence a word belongs to, in that line 'great master death and God adore'.⁵ Here we will find the meaning altogether different if we place the pause before or after the word 'death'.

<We may here observe that it is almost always improper to place *and* in the beginning of a member of a sentence, though it may be some times, though rarely, proper to begin a sentence in that manner, and then there is no danger of ambiguity.>

Another ambiguity, also, to be avoided, is that where it is difficult to know what verb the nominative case belongs to, or what noun an adjective agrees with. The ancient languages were much more liable to this ambiguity than the modern ones, as they admitted of a greater freedom in the arrangement of the words. As an example of this we take that line of Juvenal, *Nobilitas sola atque unica Virtus,*⁶ where the ambiguity is owing to the not distinguishing whether *sola* agrees with *virtus* or *nobilitas*.

This line may serve as an instance of the ambiguity proceeding from the verb not being ascertained to belong to one substantive more than another: 'In this alone beasts do the men excel', where one would be apt to think the author meant that the beasts excelled men in this alone, whereas the contrary is certainly the meaning.

The best authors very seldom fall into this error, Thucydides, Xenophon and several others; nay Dr. Clarke says he has found but one instance in all Homer. This indeed may be turned in very different ways; but as the rest is so exact this one probably proceeds from the error of some transcriber. It is wonderful no more errors of this sort have crept in during so long a tract of time, and may serve to show the surprising accuracy of that writer.

---

⁵ *Essay on Man*, I, 1.92. Pope has 'teacher', not 'master'. (Lothian.)
⁶ Juvenal, Satires, VIII, 1.20. '*The sole and only nobility is virtue.*'

Mr. Waller, again, is a remarkable instance of the defect of this quality, and as he pays very little regard to grammatical rules his sense is sometimes hardly to be come at, though this method will often serve to discover the meaning of other obscure writers. The characterists[7] are extremely free from this, and would be the book most easily construed.

A natural order of expression, free of parentheses and superfluous words, is likewise a great help towards perspicuity. In this consists what we call easy writing which makes the sense of the author flow naturally upon our mind without our being obliged to hunt backwards and forwards in order to find it. <When there are no words that are superfluous but all tend to express something by themselves which was not said before, and in a plain manner, we may call it precision; though this word is often taken to mean a stiff and affected style such as that of Pym and others of the puritan writers.> Bolingbroke especially and Swift have excelled most in this respect; accordingly we find that their writings are so plain that one half asleep may carry the sense along with him, <even though the sentence be very long, as in that in the end of his essay on virtue.> Nay if we happen to lose a word or two, the rest of the sentence is so naturally connected with it as that it comes into our mind of its own accord.

On the other hand, writers who do not observe this rule often become so obscure that their meaning is not to be discovered without great attention and being altogether awake. Shaftesbury sometimes runs into this error by endeavouring to throw a great deal together before us.

Writings of this sort have a great deal of the air of translations from an other language, where a certain stiffness of expression and repetition of synonymous words is very apt to be gone into.

Short sentences are generally more perspicuous than long ones, as they are more easily comprehended in one view; but when we intend to study conciseness we should avoid the unconnected way of writing which we are then very apt to

---

[7] *Sic: Characteristics?* Obviously Smith refers to one book, and Shaftesbury's *Characteristics* seems to be what he intended. (Lothian.)

run into, and at the same time is of all others the most obscure. The reason of this is that when we study short sentences and render our expressions concise as well as our sentences. But precision and a close adherence to a just expression are very consistent with a long sentence, and a short sentence may very possibly want both. Sallust, Tacitus and Thucydides are the most remarkable in this way; and it is proper to observe that concise expressions and short-turned periods are proper only for historians who narrate facts barely as they are, or those who write in the didactic style. The three historians we mentioned are accordingly the chief who have followed this manner of writing. It is very improper for orators or public speakers, as their design is to rouse the passions, which are not affected by a plain simple style, but require the attacks of strong and perhaps exaggerated expressions. No didactic writer has invariably adhered to this style though it be proper to them, unless Aristotle, who never once deviates from it in his whole works, whereas others often run out into oratorical declamation.

What are generally called ornaments or flowers in language, as allegorical, metaphorical and such like expressions are very apt to make ones style dark and perplexed. Studying much to vary the expression leads one also frequently into a dungeon of metaphorical obscurity. The Lord Shaftesbury, is of all authors I know, the most liable to this error. In the third volume of his works, talking of meditating and reflecting within oneself, he contrives an innumerable number of names for it, each more dark than another, as 'self-conversation', 'forming a plurality in the same person' etc. In an other place he says that his head was the dupe of his heart, where another would have said that he was so intent on obtaining a certain [thing] that he could not help thinking he would obtain it. But it is plain this author had it greatly in view to go out of the common road in his writings and to dignify his style by never using common phrases or even names for things, and we see hardly any expression in his works but what would appear absurd in common conversation. To such a length does he carry this that he won't even call *men* by their own names. Moses is the 'Jewish lawgiver', Xenophon 'the young warrior', Plato 'the philosopher of noble birth'; and in his treatise written expressly to prove the being of God he never almost uses that word but the 'supreme being or mind', or 'he that knows all things,' etc.

The frequent use of Pronouns is also not agreeable to perspicuity, as it makes [us] look to what they refer to. They are, however, proper where the noun whose place they supply is not the chief or emphatical one in the sentence. But in that case the repetition of the word itself gives greater strength and energy to the sentence.

We might here insist on this, as well as proper variation of the form of a sentence and how far our language could admit of it, but this, as well as many other grammatical parts we must altogether pass over as tedious and unentertaining, and proceed to give an estimate of our own language compared with others. In order to this it will be proper to premise somewhat with regard to the origin and design of language in the general.

READING V[8]

Lecture 7, Wednesday, 1 December, 1762

Besides those tropes and figures as they are called, of which we treated in the last lecture, there are others that consist either in the meaning the word is taken in or in the arrangement of the words. The first they call *figuræ verborum*, the second *figuræ sententiarum*.[9] When we use a feminine for a

---

[8] From Adam Smith's 'Lectures on Rhetoric and Belles Lettres', transcribed by John Lothian, published by Thomas Nelson (1963), pp. 29–35.

[9] *Figura verborum* and *figura sententiarum* literally translate to 'form of the words' and 'form of the intention (or purpose)', but these terms, from the ancient Greek rhetorical discourses, were expanded by Cicero and Quintilian to refer to language that departs from ordinary language in its attempt to provide a form to the thoughts. *Figura verborum* does this through the use of words (for instance rhetorical repetitions, phonetic matching, asyndeton, etc.), while *figura sententiarum* does this through figures of thought (for instance prolepsis, the rhetorical question, personification, etc). The *figura* are distinct from *tropes* in that they are not pre-made, it is a rhetorical art to find the form to translate an idea into moving language.

masculine or even give another gender to a neuter, this is a *figura verborusm*. *Figura sententiarum*, on the other hand, are such as imperative, interrogative or exclamatory phrases. But these as we observed above give no beauty of their own, they only are agreeable and beautiful when they suit the sentiment and express in the neatest manner the way in which the speaker is affected. When the common form of speech well enough describes the thing we want to make known or sufficiently communicates our sentiments, yet perhaps it does not express clearly and with sufficient life the manner we ourselves regard it — if in this case the figurative way of speaking is more suited to our purpose, then it surely ought to be used preferably to the other. But we may observe that the most beautiful passages are generally the most simple. That passage of Demosthenes[10] in which he describes the confusion at Athens after the battle of Elateia is reckoned by Longinus[11] the most sublime of all his writings; and yet there is not one figure or trope through the whole of it. Very often the figures seem to diminish rather than add to the beauty of an excellent passage. Two of the most beautiful passages in all Pope's works are those in which he describes the state of mind of an untaught Indian,[12] and the other in which he considers the various ranks and orders of beings in the Universe.[13]

Lo the Poor Indian whose untutored mind
Sees God in clouds and hears him in the wind, etc.

The words 'watery waste' had been better exchanged for 'ocean' but that the rhyme required them.

Behold above around and underneath
all nature full and bursting into birth, etc.

---

[10] Demosthenes, *De Corona*, 169. (Lothian.)
[11] Longinus, *On the Sublime*, X, 7. (Lothian.)
[12] Pope, *Essay on Man*, I, 11.99ff. (Lothian.)
[13] Ibid. I, 11.233–4. Pope's text reads:
'See, thro' this air, this ocean, this earth,
All matter quick, and bursting into birth' (Lothian).

In the latter of these there is not any one figurative expression, and the few there are in the other are no advantage to it.

On the other hand there is nowhere more use made of figures than in the lowest and most vulgar conversation, The Billingsgate language is full of it. Sancho Panza, and people of his stamp who speak in proverbs, always abound in figures. For we may observe that a proverb always contains one, at least, and often two metaphors.

Upon the whole then, figures of speech give no beauty to style: it is when the expression is agreeable to the sense of the speaker and his affection that we admire it.

But the same sentiment may often be naturally and agreeably expressed and yet the manner be very different, according to the circumstances of the author. The same story may be considered either as plain matter of fact without design to excite our compassion; or in a moving way, or lastly in a jocose manner, according to the point in which it is connected with the author. There are a variety of characters which we may equally admire as equally good and amiable, and yet these may be very different. It would then be very absurd to blame that of a good-natured man because he wanted the severity of a more rigid one. A man of superior sense and penetration is not to be condemned because he gives his assent to the opinion of the company with the same ease as one of a more soft temper and of less parts (whose character for this reason very often acceptable) will do. Other characters all very commendable, cannot be blamed because they want some perfections we are apt to admire, for these perhaps are not at all consistent with them, and can hardly meet in the same person. The consideration of this variety of characters affords us often no small entertainment, it forms one of the chief pleasures of social life, and few are so foolish as to blame it or consider it as any defect.

In the same manner the various styles, instead of being condemned for the want of beauties perhaps incompatible with those they possess, may be considered as good in their kind and suited to the circumstance of the author. This observation confirms what we before observed that the expression ought to be suited to the mind of the author, for this is chiefly governed by the circumstances he is placed in. <The style of an author is generally of the same stamp as

their character. Thus the ... of ... and the ... of the flowery modesty of Addison, the pert and flippant insolence of Warburton, ... of ... appear evident in their works and point the very character of the man.>

A didactic writer and a historian seldom make use of the bolder figures, which an orator frequently introduces with advantage. The end they have in view is different and so the means by which they hope to accomplish that end must be so too.

It is here to be observed that an orator or didactic writer has two parts in his work. In the one he lays down his proposition and in the other he brings his proof of that proposition. An historian on the other hand has only one part, to wit, the proposition. He barely tells you the facts, and if he has any thing as a proof of it, it is only a quotation from some other author in a note or parenthesis. From this it is that though the circumstances of an orator and a didactic writer are very different, there is a much greater resemblance betwixt their styles than even betwixt the style of the latter and the historian's. The orator and historian are indeed in very different circumstances. The business of the one is barely to narrate the facts which are often very distant from his time and in which he is, or ought to be, and endeavours to appear, noways interested. The orator, again, treats of subjects he or his friends are nearly concerned in; it is his business therefore to appear—if he is not really—deeply concerned in the matter, and uses all his art to prove what he is engaged in. Their styles are no less different. The orator insists on every particular, exposes it in every point of view, and sets of every argument in every shape it can bear. What the historian would have said barely and in one sentence by this means is brought into a long series of different views of the same argument. The orator frequently will exclaim on the strength of the argument, the justice of the cause, or any thing else that tends to support the thing he has in view; and this, too, in his own person. The historian, again, as he is in no pain what side seems the justest, but acts as if he were an impartial narrator of the facts, so he uses none of these means to affect his readers, he never dwells on any circumstance, nor has he any use for insisting on arguments, as he does not take part with either side, and for the same reason he never uses any exclamations in his own person. When he does so we say he departs from the character of the historian and assumes that of the orator. Amongst the ancient historians I remember but three instances of such exclamations in the first person: one in Veleius Paterculus on the death, and the other in Florus on the eloquence, of Cicero; the third is in Tacitus' life of Agricola, at the end, on the character of that Roman. <Virgil has but three exclamations in the Aeneid, one on the love of Dido, another on the death of Pallas, a third on that of Nisus and Euryalus, *Felices animae si quid mea carmina possunt*.[14]>

The didactic writer, as his circumstances are nearer to that of the orator, so their styles bear a much greater resemblance to each other. The orator often lays aside the dictatorial style and barely offers his arguments in a plain modest manner, especially when his discourse is directed to those of greater judgment and higher rank than himself.

The didactic writer sometimes assumes an oratorial style though it may be questioned whether this be altogether so proper. Cicero often does so. Not only in those writings which are wrote in the manner of dialogue, but where he speaks in his own person, he often runs out into oratorial exclamations, and dwells on the same argument, and repeats it in different manners. Most other writers of this sort often do so as well as he. Aristotle amongst the ancients, and Dr. Mandeville[15] among the moderns, are perhaps the only two who have adhered closely to this peculiar style of a didactic writer. They trust solely to the strength of their arguments,

---

[14] Velleius paterculus, II 66 or II, 129–31; Florus, II, 13, 94 (death of *Julius Caesar*); Tacitus, *Agricola*, 45, 3: Virgil, *Aeneid*, IV, ll. 65–7 or 408–12; X 1.507; IX, 1.1.466. The line quoted should read *Fortunati ambo*. (Lothian.) It is from Virgil's description of the death of Nisus and Euryalus. Dr. Daniel Carpenter notes that while it is presumably the student transcriber's misquote, the mistaken line still transcribes in perfect hexameter (demonstrating considerable proficiency in Latin, if not a perfect recollection of the Aeneid).

[15] Prof. Lothian opts for Mandeville here, although J.C. Bryce opts for Machiavelli, noting that Hand B replaces Hand A's deleted 'Dr. Mandeville' with 'Machiavelli'.

and the ingenuity and newness of their thoughts and discoveries, to gain the assent of their readers.

Such is the variety of styles that those which appear the most like have still a great difference. No two styles have a greater connection than a plain and a simple one, but they are far from being the same. A plain man is one who pays no regard to the common civilities and forms of good breeding. He gives his opinion bluntly and affirms without condescending to give any reason for his doing so; and if he mentions any sort of a reason it is only to shew how evident and plain a matter it was and expose the stupidity of the others in not perceiving it as well as he. <He is not at all ruffled by contradiction or any irritation whatever, but is at pains to shew that this proceeds from his confidence in his own superior sense and judgment. He never gives way either to joy or grief; such affections would be below the dignity and complacence of mind which he affects. Compassion finds little room in his breast; admiration does not at all suit his wisdom; contempt is more agreeable to his self-sufficient imperious temper.> He is not at all sedulous to please: on the contrary he affects a sort of austerity and hardness of behaviour, so that when the common civilities of behaviour would be the most natural and easy manner, he industriously avoids them. He is so far from affecting any graces or civilities that he affects the contrary, and renders himself more severe than his nature would naturally lead him to be. <He despises the fashion in every point and neither conforms himself to it in dress, in language, nor manners, but sticks by his own downright way.> Wit would ill-suit his gravity. He is more apt to think that others have ill motives even when they act well than that they are only in a mistake and do not err knowingly when they act amiss. <He affirms without mitigation or apology.> In ordinary conversation he thinks it enough to support what he says that it is his opinion, and is at no pains to enquire into those of others.

Such a character is what clergymen generally assume, and those come to age. It does well enough in those of superior abilities, who have had greater opportunities than common, or longer experience, but young men generally avoid it. Modesty and diffidence are more suited to their years than the assuming arrogance of this character; which even though accompanied with age and knowledge renders the possessor rather the object of our respect and esteem than of our love.

The simple man again, is not indeed studious to appear with all the outward marks of civility and breeding that he sees others of a more disingenuous temper generally put on; but then, when they naturally express his real sentiments, he readily uses them. He appears always willing to please, when this desire does not lead him to act disingenuously. At other times the modesty and affability of his behaviour, his being always willing to comply with customs that don't look affected, plainly shew the goodness of his heart. He is not over ready to give his opinion, and when he does, it 'tis with that unaffected modesty which displays itself in all his behaviour, and in nothing more than in his conversation, where his diffidence of his own judgment leads him to offer all the reasons he has to be of that mind to shew that he does not assert any thing merely because it is his opinion. Contempt never enters into his mind; he is more ready to think well than meanly both of the parts and the conduct of others. His own goodness of heart makes him never suspect others of disingenuity. He is always open to conviction and is not at all irritated by others contradicting him: but the reason of this is not any stubbornness but the diffidence he entertains of his own capacity. <This leads him to speak very often in the first person to shew the mean opinion he has of himself, and sometimes to childish prating.> He is more given to admiration and pity, joy, pity, grief, and compassion than the contrary affections, they suit well with the softness of his temper. This temper is what we often find in young men and in them is very agreeable. Old men are generally not so apt to be of this character. It renders one more an object of love and affection than regard and esteem.

When the characters of a plain and a simple man are so different we may naturally expect that the style they express themselves in will be far from being the same. Swift may serve as an instance of a plain style and Sir Wm. Temple of a simple one. Swift never gives any reason for his opinions but affirms them boldly without the least hesitation; and when one expects a reason he meets with nothing but such expressions as, 'I have always been of opinion that', or 'because it seems to me'. This we find he does in the beginning of his *Considerations on the Present State of Affairs*. He is so far from studying the ornaments of language that he affects to leave them out even when natural; and in this way he often throws out pronouns etc, that are necessary to make the sentence full but would at the same time lead him into the uniformity of cadence which he industriously avoids. This however makes his style very close, no word can be passed over without notice; every other one must be strongly accented to draw the attention of the hearer, for a word lost would spoil the whole. This makes us read his works with more life and emphasis than those of most authors. In Shaftesbury and Bolingbroke, or others who study this uniformity of cadence, there are many superfluous words which we huddle together as being of very small importance to the sense of the period. He never introduces (in his grave works) any sort of figure; and that for the same reason as he avoids harmony and smoothness of cadence. He never expresses any passion but affirms with a dictatorial gravity.

Temple, on the other hand, is not anxious about ornaments; but when they are natural he does not reject them. His style has neither the hardness of Swifts nor the laboured regularity of Shaftesbury. The most common and received opinions he never [expresses] but the most [blank] manner possible, as that saying that wit and solid judgment are seldom or ever found together, which he brings in his character of the Dutch nation.[16] He does not avoid a figurative style when agreeable to his subject, as in the comparison betwixt the life of a merchant and a soldier, <in which there are a great many antitheses. These Swift never uses in his grave works, they savour too much of the paradox, that is of wit, to suit his gravity.> He uses more obsolete words here than we would expect in a writer of his age. This we never find in Swift. The knowledge of the world which <he> affects and which he chiefly employs to satirize it and turn it to ridicule, will not allow him to use anything that is out of the present taste. But Temple is led to them by the notion that every

---

[16] *Observations upon the United Provinces of the Netherlands*, ed. Clark, Cambridge, Ch. 4, passim. (Lothian.)

thing belonging to our forefathers has more simplicity than those of our times, as we they were a more simple and honest set of men. His love of a modest simple style leads him (but in a different manner from Swift) to use the first person very often, as well as to run into 'prating and quibble'. The description he gives of [blank] may serve as an instance of both the former. When he says, 'The earth of Holland is better than the air, the love of interest stronger than the love of honour,'[17] it is a mere quibble on the words 'earth' and 'profit', 'air' and 'honour'. Xenophon and most other writers of this sort as well as he, abound in jokes we are surprised to find in such grave writers.

READING VI[18]

Lecture 8, Friday, 3 December, 1762

Having in the foregoing lecture made some observations on tropes and figures and endeavoured to shew that it was not in their use, as the ancient rhetoricians imagined, that the beauties of style consisted, I pointed out what it was that really gave beauty to words neatly and properly expressed the thing to be described, and conveyed the sentiment the author entertained of it and desired to communicate to his hearers, by then the expression had all the beauty language was capable of bestowing on it. I endeavoured to shew, also, that the form of the style was not to be confined to any particular point. The view of the author and the means he takes to accomplish that end must vary the style not only in describing different objects or delivering different opinions but even when these are the same in both; as the sentiment will be different, so will the style also. Besides this, I endeavoured to shew that when all other circumstances are alike the character of the author must make the style different. One of grave cast of mind will describe an object in very different way from one of more levity, a plain man will

---

[17] Ibid., p. 115. (Lothian.)
[18] From Adam Smith's 'Lectures on Rhetoric and Belles Lettres', transcribed by John Lothian, published by Thomas Nelson (1963), pp. 36-43.

have a style very different from that of a simple man. There is, however, no one particular which we esteem, but many are equally agreeable. Extreme moroseness and gravity, such that no risible objects will in the least affect, would not be admired: neither would one of such levity that the smallest incident would make lose himself. But it is not in the middle point betwixt these two characters that an agreeable one is alone to be found, many others that partake more or less of the two extremes are equally the objects of our attention. In the same way it is with regard to a spirited and silly behaviour, and every two other opposite extremes in the characters of men.

These characters, though all good and agreeable, must nevertheless, as they are different, be expressed in very different styles, all of which may be very agreeable. And here likewise the rule may be applied, that one should stick to his natural character. A gay man should not endeavour to be grave, nor the grave man to be gay, but each should regulate that character and manner that is natural to him and hinder it from running into that vicious extreme to which he is most inclined.

This difference of style arising from the character of the author, I endeavoured to illustrate by comparing the styles of two celebrated English writers, Swift and Sir Wm. Temple; the one as an example of the plain style, and the other of a simple one. Both are very good writers. Swift, as I observed, is remarkable for his propriety and precision, the other is not perhaps so very accurate, but he is perhaps as entertaining and much more instructive. I shall now proceed to make some farther observation on the style of Dr. Swift.

There is perhaps no writer whose works are more generally read than his, and yet it has been very late that very few in this country particularly understand his real worth. He is read with the same view and the same expectations as we read *Tom Brown*.[19] They are considered as writers

---

[19] Tom Brown (1663–1704), an amusing light-weight satirist and translator. His *Letters for the Dead to the Living* and *Amusements Serious and Comical* (1700) are his chief works. His name is underlined in the manuscript. (Lothian.)

just of same class. Swifts graver works are never almost read; they are looked upon as silly and trifling, and his other works are read merely for their humour.

We shall therefore endeavour to find out what are the causes of this general taste. And first: Swift's sentiments in religious matters are not at all suitable to those which for some time past have prevailed in this country. He is indeed no friend to tyranny either religious or civil; he expresses his abhorrence to them on many occasions. But then he never has such warm exclamations for civil or religious liberty as are now generally in fashion. This would not suit his character, the plain man he affects to appear would never be subject to such strong admiration. The levity of mind as well as freedom of thought now in fashion demands warmer and more earnest expressions than he ever allows himself.

Another circumstance that will tend to confirm this opinion is that the thoughts of most men of genius in this country have of late (inclined) to abstract and speculative reasonings which perhaps tend very little to the bettering of our practice. <Even the practical sciences of Politics and Morality or Ethics have of late been treated too much in a speculative manner.> These studies Swift seems to have been rather entirely ignorant of, or what I am rather inclined to believe, did not hold them to be of great value. His general character as a plain man would lead him to be of this way of thinking; he would be more inclined to prosecute what was immediately beneficial. Accordingly we find that all his writings are adapted to the present time, either in ridiculing some prevailing vice or folly or exposing some particular character. We cannot now enter altogether into the true spirit of these; and besides as I said such confined thoughts do not suit the present taste which delights only in general and abstract speculations.

But his language may possibly have brought about the general disregard for his serious works as much as any other part of his character. We in this country are most of us very sensible that the perfection of language is very different from that we commonly speak in. The idea we form of a good style is almost contrary to that which we generally hear. Hence it is that we conceive the farther one's style is removed from the common manner, it is so much the nearer to purity and the perfection we have in view. Shaftesbury, who keeps at a vast distance from the language we commonly meet with, is for this reason universally admired. Thomson, who perhaps was of the same opinion himself, is equaled with Milton, who, amongst his other beauties, has this also, that he does not affect forced expressions even when he is most sublime. Swift on the other hand, who is the plainest as well as the most proper and precise of all the English writers, is despised as nothing out of the common road: each of us thinks he would have wrote as well. And our thoughts of the language give us the same idea of the substance of his writings. But it does not appear that this opinion is well grounded. There are four things that are requisite to make a good writer: first, that he have a complete knowledge of his subjects; secondly, that he should arrange all the parts of his subject in their proper order; thirdly, that he paint or describe the ideas he has of these several in the most proper and expressive manner—this is the art of painting or imitation (or at least we may call it so).

Now we will find that Swift has attained all these perfections. All his works shew a complete knowledge of his subject. He does not indeed ever introduce any thing foreign to his subject, in order to display his knowledge of his subject; but then he never omits any thing necessary. His *Rules for Behaviour* and his *Directions for a Servant*[20] shew a knowledge of both those opposite characters that could not have been attained but by the closest attention continued for many years. <It would have been impossible for any one who had not given such attention to allege so many particulars.> The same is apparent in all his political works, insomuch that one would imagine his thoughts had been altogether turned that way.

One who has such a complete knowledge of what he treats will naturally arrange it in the most proper order. This we see Swift always does. There is no part that we can think would have been better disposed of. That he paints but each

---

[20] Probably *A Treatise on Good Manners and Good Breeding*, and *Directions to a Servant*. 'Directions' cancelled in the MS and 'rules' substituted. (Lothian).

thought in the best and most proper manner and with the greatest strength of colouring must be visible to any one at first sight. <That he does this when he speaks in his own person we observed already and that he does so when he takes in the character of another is sufficiently evident from his *Gulliver*.>

Now that a writer who has all these qualities in such perfection should not make the best style for expressing himself in, with propriety and precision, cannot be imagined. Notwithstanding of all this, perhaps for the reasons already shown, his graver works are not much regarded. It is his talent for ridicule that is most commonly and, I believe, most justly admired. We shall therefore consider how far this talent is agreeable to the general character we have already given of him, and whether or not he has prosecuted it with the same exactness as the other subjects we mentioned. But before we enter upon this it will be necessary to make a few previous observations on this talent.

Whatever we see that is great or noble excites our admiration and amazement; and whatever is little or mean on the other excites our contempt.<This Leibniz, and, after him, Mr. Locke supposed to be excited by the viewing of some mean object; but that this is not the case will appear from what follows.> A great object never excites our laughter, neither does a mean one, simply as being such. It is the blending and joining of those two ideas which alone causes that emotion.

<The foundation of ridicule is either when what is in most respects grand, or pretends to be so, or is expected to be so has something mean or little in it, or when we find something that is really mean with some pretensions and marks of grandeur.> Now this may happen either when an object which is in most respects a grand one, is represented to us and described as mean, or *e contra* when a grand object is found in company as it were with others that are mean; or *e contra* when our expectation is disappointed and what we imagined was either grand or mean turns out to be the reverse. These different combinations of ideas afford each a different form or manner of ridicule.

If we represent an object which we are apt to conceive as a grand one, or as of no dignity, and turn its qualities into the contrary, the mixture of the ideas excites our laughter though neither of them separately would do so. Hence come the ridicule conveyed to us by burlesque or mock heroic compositions. The circumstances a thing is in, also, if their be any great contradiction betwixt the objects, for the same reason excites our laughter. A tall man is no object of laughter, neither is a little, but a very tall man amongst a number of dwarfs, like Gulliver amongst the Lillyputians, or a little man amongst a set of very tall men as the same Gulliver in Brobdignag, appear ridiculous. There is no real foundation for laughter here, but the odd association of grand and mean or little ideas. <In this and similar cases it is the group of figures, and no individual one which is the object of our ridicule.> <The ridicule in the *Rape of the Lock* proceeds from the ridiculousness of the characters themselves, but that of the *Dunciad* is owing altogether to the circumstances the persons are placed in. Any two men, Pope and Swift themselves, would look as ridiculous as Curl and Lintot, if they were described running the same races.> We laugh against our will at the employment of Socrates when we see him in the *Clouds* of Aristophanes measuring the length of a flea's leap by the length of the same flea's foot, or suspended in a bucket making observations.[21] If this philosopher had been so employed he would have appeared ridiculous, and the great contrariety of the ideas makes the very supposition appear so.

<The wit of some of the French comedians as [blank] is founded in this principle. The Lover in Fougu is no ways ridiculous but by the circumstances.> The Italian comedians, at Paris, as they are called, as soon as any grave or solemn tragedy appears on the theatre, give the same play, that is the same incidents, applied to some very opposite character. Generals and Emperors become burghers or turn mechanics. The ridicule here is owing to the contrast between the high ideas connected with the incidents we have seen attendant on great characters, and the same incidents happening to persons of a rank so much lower. When what we expect to find great and noble turns out otherwise we are in the same

---

[21] Aristophanes, *Clouds*, ll. 143–52; ibid., ll. 218ff. (Lothian.)

manner moved to laughter, and *e contra*. A sow wallowing in the mire is certainly a loathsome object, but no one would laugh at it, as it is agreeable to the nature of the beast. But if he saw the sow afterwards in a drawing room, the case would be altered. On the other hand, a lean, poor-looking, raw-boned horse excite's ones laughter as <that noble animal seems to lay claim to our admiration>, we expect something great and noble in the appearance of that animal. One would not laugh at a bad prospect, as there is no contradiction in supposing one, unless we had been made to expect a fine one, but we laugh at a bad picture because we expect that art is exercised in some noble manner.

'Tis from such combinations chiefly that ridicule proceeds; we may laugh, too, at things we contemn, but in a different manner. A coxcomb walking on the Street and looking around him to see those about admiring him as he expects, is a subject of laughter to the graver sort: but then this laughter that proceeds from an object we contemn is evidently mixt with somewhat of anger. But if this same coxcomb should slip a foot and fall into the kennel, the grave gentlemen would laugh but from a different motive, at the ridiculous plight such a fine fellow was in; which was the very condition they at their hearts would have wished him. Some philosophers as [blank] observing that laughter proceeds sometimes from contempt, have made it the original of all ridiculous perceptions. But we may frequently laugh at objects that are not at all contemptible. A tall man amongst a number of little men or *e contra* makes us laugh but we don't contemn either. Things that have no sort of connection, but where the ideas we have are strangely contradictory, excite our laughter. I remember once a mouse running across the area of a chapel spoilt the effect of an excellent discourse. Any such trivial accidents excite our laughter when they happen at any solemn or important work, as a funeral. 'Tis for this reason that we are diverted with those phrases that we are accustomed to connect in our imagination with noble objects, when we meet with them applied to mean and trifling ones. Hence comes the ridiculousness of parodies (or applying whole passages of an author by a sort of translation to subjects of a very different sort, and centos where single phrases are applied.) The Cento of Apuleius,[22] where the grave and chaste Virgil is made to speak in his own words on a very different subject and in not very chaste language, no where makes us laugh but in the story of the marriage. <All the ridicule of Scarron's *Virgil Travesti* in the same manner proceeds from the grave and solemn adventures of Æneas being told in the most ridiculous language and trivial, mean expressions.> The modern Latin poets, Vida, Sanazzaro, etc. are all parodies on some of the ancient Latin poets. These, not being on trivial subjects, but such as are equally important, do not excite our laughter but are rather tedious and wearisome. The English poets are more original: they do not usually borrow from others — such dealings would be counted no better than stealing — and for that reason are not so tiresome. The *Splendid Shilling*[23] diverts us by the ridiculous appearance Milton's language makes when used to extol the charms of a shilling. <The incongruity of the language to the Subject has also its effect here as well as in works of the contrary sort as *Virgil Travesti*.> But so far is it from being a sign of any passage's being a mean one, that a parody has been made upon it, that 'tis rather a sign of the contrary, as the more sublime and pompous a passage is, the greater the contrast will be when the phraseology is applied to trivial subjects. Thus we see the soliloquy of Hamlet, the last speech of Cato, have undergone more parodies than any others I know, and indeed make very good ones. For the same reason parodies on the Scriptures, though very profane, are at the same time very ridiculous.

<Puns, which are the lowest species of wit, are never wholly agreeable but when there is some contrast betwixt the ideas they excite: a mere quibble is never agreeable.>

There are two species of comic writing derived from two species of ridiculous circumstances. The one is when characters ridiculous in themselves are described, and the

---

[22] An error for Ausonius, *Cento Nuptialis* (Loeb ed., vol. I, pp. 370–93). (Lothian.)
[23] *The Splendid Shilling* (1705), by John Philips. (Lothian.)

other when characters that have nothing ridiculous in themselves are described in ridiculous circumstances. The ... in the ... of ... is an instance ... of the former, and the lover of ... in Le Fougueux of ...[24] is an instance of the latter. The whole of Congreve's wit consists in the ridiculousness of his similes, as his comparing two persons bespattering one another to two apples roasting, or the young lady newly come to town, gaping with amazement, he compares her wide opened mouth to the gate of her father's house.

It is proper to be observed that of all these species of ridicule, Burlesque, Doggerel, Mock Heroic, Parodies, Centos, Puns, Quibbles and even that sort of comedy which ridicules characters not from their real defects but from the circumstances they are brought into, are all of the buffoonish sort and unworthy of a gentleman who has had a regular education; and whenever such a one exercises his wit in this manner, he lays aside that character to assume that of a buffoon at least for the time he does so. The only species of ridicule which is true and genuine wit is that where real foibles and blemishes in the characters or behaviour of men are exposed to our view in a ridiculous light. This is altogether consistent with the character of a gentleman, as it tends to the reformation of manners and the benefit of mankind.

<The objects of ridicule are two: either those which, affecting to be grand, or being expected to be so, are mean, or being grand in some of their parts are mean in others; or such as, pretending etc. to beauty, are deformed.>

READING VII[25]

Lecture 26, Monday, 31 January, 1763

In the last lecture I endeavoured to give you some notion of the manner and spirit of the Deliberative orations of

---

[24] Manuscript has many blanks. (Lothian.)
[25] From Adam Smith's 'Lectures on Rhetoric and Belles Lettres', transcribed by John Lothian, published by Thomas Nelson (1963), pp. 148-156.

Demosthenes. Besides them there have no Deliberative orations of any of the Greek Orators come down to our time. [...]

We shall therefore proceed to the Deliberative orations of Cicero which are the chief ones that remain in the Latin language. These we shall find are of a very different genius from those of Demosthenes. They have a certain gravity and affectation of dignity which those of the latter want. It is commonly said the Latin is a grave and solemn language, and much more so than the Greek, which is said to be a merry and sprightly one. It were easy to shew that all languages, Greek and Latin not excepted, are equally ductile and equally accommodated to all different tempers. The style, indeed, of the Latin authors has much more of solemnity and affected dignity and ornament than that of the Greek authors. The difference betwixt style and language is often not attended to, and has not been observed by several authors, though they be in themselves very different, and to this it is owing that what is true only of the style of the writers has been ascribed to the nature and temper of the language itself.

That we may better understand the particular temper and genius of Cicero's manner of writing and the causes of it, it will be proper to make some observations on the state of the Roman commonwealth and the temper of the people at the time he wrote, which, though one of the most important parts of history, is generally too little insisted on by authors, and understood by very few.

Before this time the great distinctions of the people had been in a great measure abolished; all magistracies were now become attainable by the whole of the multitude. Those magistracies, which were formerly the peculiar province of the Patricians, were laid upon to every one. The Senatorial dignity, the office of the Praetor, Censor, Ædile etc. (which were called the Curule magistracies), were no longer confined to the old Patricians. The factions of the State were formerly those of the Patricians and Plebeians. The differences and contentions which sprung up after the expulsion of the Kings all arose from the rivalship of those two bodies. But by these continued contentions, the magistracies, and all of power and profit were by degrees opened to the people.

From these immense riches and immense power and interest were often acquired by individuals, both of the Patrician and the nobler Plebeian families. There are many instances of immense fortunes raised by the oppression of those who were under the power and direction of the different officers. The proconsul Verres[26] may serve as an instance of this; and there are many of as extraordinary and immense power obtained by those who instead of oppressing chose to ingratiate themselves with those whom they had under their subjection, — Marius, Cinna etc. The authority of the Senate was now, indeed, little more than nominal: they could make no laws nor transact any business of importance without the consent and approbation of the people. Some few offices remained at their disposal: but their approbation to the decrees of the people was in most cases no more than a mere form. There had indeed been some attempts to reinstate the Patricians in their former authority. Sulla even made laws to this effect; but the alteration made by them was so great that they were allowed to subsist no longer than the power of him who introduced them. By this means the old parties of Patrician and Plebeian were at an end. It was now as much the interest of the chief men of the Plebeians to support the authority of the Senate and other dignified offices as it had formerly been to curb them. The power or wealth they had acquired, or had a prospect of acquiring by them, were sufficient motives for them to promote the authority of those offices, and the depression of those who were subject to them. This joint interest formed a division amongst the citizens somewhat similar but considerably different from the old one. On the one side were all the richer and more powerful of the citizens, whether Patrician or Plebeians, all who had either enjoyed the offices of power and profit, or those who had a prospect of reaping those advantages — that is, today, the people of fashion, all who would go under the denomination of Gentlemen. These were called Optimates, a word signifying no more than that they were, as we would say, the better sort, people of fashion. The other faction was

---

[26] Not pro-consul but pro-praetor (Sicily, 73–71 BC). (Lothian.)

those of the Plebeians who had not power nor riches to make them considerable nor any hopes of arriving at those offices which would make it in their power to obtain them. These were the lowest most despicable people imaginable, supported chiefly by the donations of the nobles. They were the rabble and mob, and a most wretched and miserable set of men imaginable. These would for their own safety oppose the oppression and extortion of the nobles, and attach themselves to those who, to gain power and weight in the commonwealth, courted the favour of this order. The method of these men, who from their attachment to the populace were called Populares, was to propose laws for the equal division of lands and the distributing of corn at the publick charge, or else by largesses and bounties bestowed out of their own private fortune. Of this sort were Clodius, Marius and others.

The effects, therefore, of the communication of the magistracies and the laying them open to all the people were very different at Rome from what they were at Athens. Neither the territory of the commonwealth nor the authority of the magistrates was so considerable as to put it in the power of those who filled the offices of state to acquire any extraordinary riches, and consequently gave them less opportunity of courting the favour of the multitude with success. By this means the magistracies continued open to all those who had merit enough to deserve them and gained the favour of their fellow citizens. The inequality of fortune was not so great as to make any distinction amongst the citizens. Five talents was reckoned a great estate for an Athenian citizen; for we find Demosthenes reproaching his rival Æschines[27] with not having celebrated with sufficient magnificence some public show, 'for' says he 'you can not plead poverty in your defence as you was then worth above five talents'. A hundred times that would have been but a very moderate fortune at Rome. And Demosthenes' also mentions

---

[27] Demosthenes, *De Corona*, 312. Smith would appear to be inaccurate in 1) speaking of Aeschines as celebrating a public show; 2) making the sum five talents, Demosthenes says he had received two from another source. (Lothian.)

that his brother-in-law would have been one of the richest
men in Athens as his father left him fifty-two talents. The
poorest citizens might here by trade raise themselves fortunes equal to those of the most wealthy. As there was therefore no considerable distinction of fortune, so there was
properly but one rank of citizens: the highest were citizens
and no more, and the lowest had the same privilege. In
Rome, on the other hand, the great power and immense
wealth which were attendant on all the chief offices of the
State soon destroyed that equality which the communication
of the magistracies meant to establish. The people was therefore divided into two factions, that of the Optimates and that
of the Populares. The first comprehended all those who had
either enjoyed, or had a reasonable expectation of enjoying,
the magistracies; that is, the few remaining old Patricians
and all the noble Plebeian families, and those who had
power or interest to advance themselves. In the other were
all the Plebeians who were not noble nor had any expectations of raising themselves to offices by which they might
attain power or riches. These (as I said) were a most
wretched and destitute set of men; they depended for their
very subsistence first, on the liberality of the candidates in
their largesses at elections, which were indeed often pro-
hibited and could not afterwards be publicly avowed. But it
was a vain attempt to hinder the people from accepting of
such presents for their votes, or the candidates from
endeavouring to carry their elections by that means. Or
secondly, they depended on the distributions of corn or other
necessaries which were made by the public either for no
price or at a low one. There was here no middle rank betwixt
those who had the greatest wealth and power and those who
were in the most abject poverty and dependence. The knights
in the earlier periods were a sort of middle betwixt the
Plebeians and the Patricians and somewhat restrained the
extravagancies of either. They were at this time horsemen,
Equites, and were distinguished from the rest of the people
by the manner of their service.

We may observe that knights in all countries were mere
horsemen originally, but when military service was not so
much used they have become of a very different rank. A
knight in this country is a very different person from a

dragoon. In the same manner the Roman *Equites* were at first those who composed the cavalry. But after the victory of Marius over the Cimbri,[28] they were never employed in that service. They were soon after allowed to be elected into the Senate, and from that time became of the same party with the remaining Patricians and other nobles. As there was but one order at Athens so there was properly only two orders at Rome, the great and the populace.

Besides this the Athenians and the Romans treated their favourites in a very different manner. All appearance of pride or extraordinary authority or presumption of any sort was looked on at Athens with a jealous eye. The people were offended with Alcibiades their greatest favourite, for wearing a dress somewhat more splendid than was ordinarily worn by the citizens. But the luxury of Lucullus or the splendor of Pompey were not objects of jealousy to the Romans. Though the Athenians could not allow Alcibiades to go gaily dressed, the Romans beheld without suspicion Pompey attended by the flower of the young nobility, a great part of the Senate, and the chief men of the City.

<The people never at this time opposed the growing power of their favourites, all they did was looked on with the greatest ease. The only check they met with was from the opposition and contrary endeavours of the other nobility who in the same manner strove to get to the head of affairs.>

The Nobleman of Rome would, then, find himself greatly superior to the far greater part of mankind. He would see at Rome a thousand who were his inferiors for one who was even his equal; and anywhere else there would be none would could compare with him in power or wealth. Finding himself thus superior to most about him he would contract a great opinion of his own dignity. He would have an air of superiority in all his behaviour. As he spoke generally to his inferiors he would talk in a manner becoming one in that station. Respect and deference would be what he thought his due as one of superior dignity and his behaviour would aim at approving himself to be such. His discourse would be

---

[28] In 101 B.C., Marius and Catulus defeated the Cimbri and their allies at Vercelli, near Verona. (Lothian.)

pompous and ornate, as such as appeared to be the language of a superior sort of man.

At Athens, on the other hand, the citizens were all on equal footing: the greatest and the meanest were considered as being no way distinguished, and lived and talked together with the greatest familiarity. Difference of fortune or employment did not hinder the ease and familiarity of behaviour. It is observed that there is no politeness or compliments in the *Dialogues* of Plato, whereas those of Cicero abound with them. Particularly in his dialogue *de Oratore*, the noblemen he introduces talk in the most polite manner and pay one another the greatest respect, and commend in the most complimenting style. Plato, again, introduces persons of the most unequal dignity or power in the State talking with the greatest freedom and familiarity, such as would appear very odd at this day amongst people of such different stations: and there is generally one person who roasts, teases, and exposes the others without mercy, and often with a turn of humour which would not be at this day altogether polite or even decent. In the one country the people, at least the nobles would converse and harangue with dignity, pomp, and the air of those who speak with authority to his hearers. The language of the others would be that of freedom, ease and familiarity. The one is that where the speaker is supposed to be of superior dignity and authority to his hearers, and the other is that of one who talks to his equals. Pomp and splendour suit the former well enough, but would appear presumption in the other.

These considerations may serve to explain many of the differences in the manners and style of Demosthenes and Cicero. The latter talks with the dignity and authority of a superior, and the former with the ease of an equal. Cicero, therefore, studies always to add what ever may give this appearance to his style even on the most trivial occasions; and the other talks with ease and familiarity even when he is the most earnest and vehement. <Demosthenes abounds with all the common phrases and idioms, and proverbs; Cicero, on the other hand, avoids all idiomatical turns or other expressions with the greatest care.> Cicero abounds with all those figures of speech which are thought to give dignity to language; his style is always correct and to the highest degree, with the greatest propriety of expression and the strictest observance of grammatical propriety. This makes it evident that the author conceives himself to be of importance, and dignity, for this exact and ornate style shows that every word is premeditated and that he has settled before he begun the sentence in what manner he was to conclude it. There are certain forms of speech which are peculiar to common conversation; and plainly appear to proceed from the carelessness of the speaker, who had not resolved when he begun his sentence in what manner he was to end it. These are called ἀνακολουθα i.e. unconnected, without consequence, where the one part of the sentence is of a different grammatical construction from the other. The Greek writers abound with this figure, but none more than Xenophon and Demosthenes. I shall mention an instance from each to explain the matter. In Xenophon, the sentence in Latin would run thus: *Hephaestus et Menon, quoniam sunt amici vestrum, remittite nobis.* The grammatical construction plainly would require here that he should have *Hephestum* et *Menona* etc. In the same manner, we would say in easy conversation, 'Hephestus and Menon as they are your friends, send them back to us'; or, 'Send back' etc., or, 'John or James such-a-thing, I know not what is become of him', instead of, 'I do not know', or 'I know not what is become' etc. The one we would use in conversation or familiar letter writing and the latter in a formal discourse or in writing a history. This has been much used by Demosthenes and other Greeks; but Cicero and most Latin writers have entirely rejected it, as well as almost all modern authors, as it testifies a great degree of carelessness in the speaker. The instance in Demosthenes I do not remember, but there are two places in the same sentence where the forgoing member by the means of some words would require the subsequent to have been altogether of an other form.

Again, Demosthenes' periods are for the most part short and concise without any redundancy of expression: Whereas Cicero always runs out into a long train of connected members, even on the most simple subject. And even when Demosthenes is obliged by the quantity of matter which crowds in upon him to form a long period, he never affects those ornaments of similarity, of cadence, and uniformity of length in the several members, which is so much studied by Cicero. This difference is very visible in their Deliberative orations but still more in their Judicial ones.

Again, the familiar ease with which Demosthenes writes makes him often use illustrations or examples as well as expressions that appear rather low and ludicrous. This is remarkable in his comparisons where he often compares things of the greatest importance to others of a very contrary nature. Thus he compares the [blank][29] sending a fleet to [blank][30] after it had been plundered and destroyed, to a oxer who always clapt his hand to the place where he felt the smart of the last blow, without attending to parry off the approaching ones or lay on any himself. Cicero, on the other hand, compares the most trivial things, and that, too, when he is rallying, with the most serious; as for instance, he says that the conduct of Mithridates[31] in leaving his treasure in Pontus, which, by employing the troops in plunder, gave the king himself time to escape, was like that of Medea, who, to retard the pursuit of her father, tore her brother in pieces and strewed his limbs on the sea, that she, whilst her father was employed in taking them up, might have time to escape.

These differences in the style of these orators may probably arise from the different condition of the countries in which they lived. The tempers of the men had no doubt also have had their effects. The vanity and pride, if you will call it so, which Cicero was possessed of, may perhaps have made him more ornate and pompous than the temper of his audience would have required; and on the other hand the severity and downright plainness of Demosthenes may have made him more bare and careless than even the familiarity and equality of his countrymen would have required. To this, too, it may be owing that Demosthenes is at no pains to repeat or expatiate on his subject, which Cicero, as we hinted, always studies. This much with regard to the expression and manner of writing.

---

[29] Perhaps, 'Calvus'. (Lothian.)
[30] Perhaps 'Caelius'. (Lothian.)
[31] *Pro Lege Manilia*, 22. (Lothian.)

As to the matter and the arrangement these two great orators seem to have succeeded with equal good fortune. The matter and the arrangement of Demosthenes, as we said, is almost always the same, as his design is the same and his audience favourable. Those of Cicero are more various in all these respects, but his success in adapting himself to the several exigencies of the cause is no less conspicuous.

Such then are the different manners of Demosthenes and Cicero, both adapted to the state of their country; and perhaps had they been practised in the other countries, they would have been less successful. Brutus and [blank], we are told, attempted this which they called the meek eloquence, and blamed Cicero for the unpolished and bold method of his orations. But we do not find that their success was at all comparable to that of Cicero, or of Hortensius, or of [blank], the first of which if we may believe Cicero[32] was still more florid and ornate than he; and the other appears from the fragments preserved by Quintilian[33] to have been very pretty and very florid, just like Cicero. This study of ornament and pomp was common, not only to all the Roman orators, but to the historians and the poets themselves. Thus Livy and Tacitus are much more ornate than Herodotus and Thucydides; Virgil[34] than Homer and Hesiod, Propertius than Theognis, etc.; [blank] and Lucretius, the most simple of all the Roman Poets is far more ornate than Hesiod. When this study is so general we may be well assured that it proceeded not from any peculiarity or humour of the writers, but from the nature and temper of the nation. 'Tis this ornate manner I would have you chiefly remark in Cicero. It appears indeed most in his Judicial orations. The one I shall translate is the fourth, Catalinan one. I translate it not because I in the least imagine there are any of you here who

---

[32] *Brutus*, 325ff. (Lothian.)
[33] Quintilian, IV, 2, 123; XI, I, 51; and elsewhere. (Lothian.)
[34] The Scribe has not been able to take down all the names rapidly. He pairs Propertius with Virgil against Homer and Hesiod, leave a blank to balance Theognis, and a blank after 'Theognis,etc'. It seems better to move Propertius, and Hesiod be balanced by Virgil (*Georgics*). (Lothian.)

would not understand the original, but because it would be unfair to compare an original of Cicero with a translation of Demosthenes. The occasion was when Cato and Silanus counselled the Senate to put those unworthy and abominable cities[35] to death, and Caesar and [blank][36] counselled to spare their lives, as the Senate had not, after the Sempronian law, the power of condemning to capital punishment, but to confine them for life alleging this to be a more savage and heavier punishment on courageous men. Cicero, then consul, was afraid to counsel death, least the odium should fall on him alone, but yet inclined and offered to execute the commands of the Fathers to do it. Betwixt these he hovers, and his whole oration is one continued train of tergiversation; which, though a most weak and pusillanimous temper, and which afterwards caused him to be banished for that very action, which he was afraid to avoid, yet is managed in a most artificial, ornate and elegant manner. And when in this case he is ornate, we may conceive what he must be in other cases.

---

[35] *Sic*: perhaps 'citizens' is intended. (Lothian.)
[36] Perhaps 'Tiberius Nero'. (Lothain.)

Four

Alexander Gerard (1728–1795)

Alexander Gerard was born in Abeerdeenshire on 22 February 1728. His father was a minister of the Presbyterian Church, as he later was, and as was his son, Gilbert Gerard. He entered Marischal College at the age of 12, and later went on for further degrees at the University of Aberdeen and Edinburgh. He received his licence to ministry at age 20, and by age 24 his academic reputation garnered him the offer of the position of Professor of Moral Philosophy at Marichal, upon the death of his own professor, David Fordyce. He was an active member of the literary society in Aberdeen, which included his friends Thomas Reid, George Campbell, James Beattie, and Thomas Blackwell. In 1752, Gerard was chosen to succeed Fordyce also as regent of Marischal, and it was thus that Gerard was heavily involved in the reformation of the curriculum of the college, which was ratified by the faculty in 1753. His first publication, in 1755, was a defence of this new movement in education, the influential *Plan of Education in the Marischal College and University of Aberdeen.*

In 1756, he won an essay contest on the subject of taste, sponsored by an Edinburgh improving society. Amongst the judges were Reid and Hume, and there was considerable interest in his essay, which was published in 1759, and enlarged and reprinted in 1780. The same year as his *Essay on Taste* was first published, he was ordained a Minster of the Church of Scotland, and following this, in 1760, he left his professorship of Philosophy to his student James Beattie, and accepted the Chair of Divinity at Marischal. Gerard became more involved in church affairs during this period, and became active in the defence of Christian belief especially from the thinking of David Hume, the motivation of his works *The Influence of the Pastoral Office of the Character Examined* (1760) and later *The Corruptions of Christianity Considered as Affecting its Truth* (1792). He resigned his position at Marischal in 1771 to accept the Chair of Divinity at King's College, which he held until his death on 22 February 1795. During his lifetime he published his popular *Dissertations on the Evidences and Genius of Christianity* (1766), *Essay on Genius*, the companion volume to *Taste* (1774), and two volumes of his *Sermons* (early 1780s). *A Compendious View of the Evidences of Natural and Revealed Religion* was published posthumously by his grandson in 1828.

Alexander Gerard was more widely read in his own time than subsequently, although his articulation of taste was a major influence upon the discourse surrounding the issue. A key component in the working of the human faculties of sensation, aesthetic pleasure, and judgment, taste is an important part of the moral economy. It also, in Gerard's analysis, is subject to formation. Regardless of the sensory perception, our judgment is cultivated by understanding the parts of an object of sensation, how those parts operate together, how fitted they are to the purpose of the object, how we are affected. For the purposes of rhetoric, this very much supports the new method of belles lettres, in which the judgment of texts becomes a critical exercise in the cultivation of taste and moral sentiment. Genius, of which taste is a 'necessary attendant', is the capacity of invention, which Gerard defines as the ability to associate and synthesize. In other words, genius creates order from chaos, or invents by crafting a novel synthesis of divergent parts. Gerard's idea of the working of genius bears striking similarity to Aristotle's definition of rhetoric as 'seeing the available means' in any given situation—Gerard calls genius 'the grand architect which not only chooses materials, but disposes them into a regular structure'.[1] Genius is mostly innate, but can be

---

[1] *Essay on Taste*, Part III, Sec. 2, p. 171.

learned. However, it must be assisted at every stage by taste, which certainly can be learned. As the century progressed, the close relationship between rhetorical instruction and the development of moral and aesthetic taste became clearer, beginning with Adam Smith's revisionary *Lectures on the Rhetoric and Belles Lettres* and culminating in Hugh Blair's *Lectures on Rhetoric and Belles Lettres*, but seen here at its most incisive inception.

Sources

Chalmers, Alexander, *General Biographical Dictionary, containing a historical and critical account of the lives and writings of the most eminent persons in every nation, particularly the British and Irish, from earliest accounts to the present time*, Vol. 15, 1813–17.

Wood, Paul, 'Gerard, Alexander (1728–1795)', *Oxford Dictionary of National Biography*, Ed. H.C.G. Matthew and Brian Harrison, Oxford: Oxford University Press, 2004. Online ed., Ed. Lawrence Goldman, Oct. 2009.

Wood, P.B., 'Science and the Pursuit of Virtue in the Aberdeen Enlightenment', *Studies in the Philosophy of the Scottish Enlightenment*, Ed. M.A. Stewart, Oxford Studies in the History of the Enlightenment, Oxford: Clarendon Press, 1990.

READING VIII

Of the Influence of Judgment upon Taste[2]

The completest *union* of the internal *senses*, is not of itself sufficient to form good taste, even though they be attended with the greatest delicacy of passion. They must be aided with *judgment*, the faculty which distinguishes things different, separates truth from falsehood, and compares together objects and their qualities. Judgment must indeed accompany even their most *imperfect* exertions. They do not operate, till certain qualities in objects have been perceived, discriminated from others similar, compared, and compounded. In all this, judgment is employed: it bears a part in the discernment and production of every form that strikes

---

[2] Excerpted from Alexander Gerard, *Essay on Taste, Second Edition with Corrections and Additions*, Edinburgh: A. Kincaid and J.Bell, London: A. Millar, 1776, Part II, Section II, pp. 85–92.

them. But in assisting their *perfect* energies, it has a still more extensive influence. Good sense is an indispensable ingredient in true taste, which always implies a quick and accurate perception of things as they really are.

That judgment may completely exhibit to the internal senses, the beauties and excellencies of *nature*, it measures the amplitude of things, determines their proportions, and traces out their wise construction and beneficial tendency. It uses all the methods which art and science indicate, for discovering those qualities that lie too deep spontaneously to strike the eye. It investigates the laws and causes of the works of *nature*: it compares and contrasts them with the more imperfect works of *art*; and thus supplies materials from which fancy may produce ideas, and form combinations, that will strongly affect the mental taste.

Judgment finds out the general characters of *each* art, and, by comparing them, draws conclusions concerning their relations which subsist between *different* arts. Till it has discovered these, none of them can acquire that additional power of pleasing which is imparted to them by their mutual connection.

In every art, a just performance consists of various parts, combined into one system, and subservient to one design. But, without the exercise of judgment, we cannot know whether the design is skilfully prosecuted, whether the means are well adjusted to the end, or whether every member which is introduced has a tendency to promote it.

In *music*, the *ear* immediately perceives the pleasure resulting from each principle: but *judgment*, assuming the perceptions of that organ, compares them, and by comparison determines their respective merit and due proportion. It enables the ear, from its discovery of the general relations, to distinguish with precision between invention and extravagance, to discern the suitableness or unsuitableness of the parts, and their fitness or unfitness to sustain the main subject.

In *painting*, judgment discovers the meaning of the piece; not only remotely, as it is the instrument of that previous knowledge which is necessary for understanding it; but also more immediately, as, from structure and relation of the parts, it infers the general design, and explains their subserviency to the main end of the whole. It compares the imitation with its exemplar, and sees its likeness. It is judgment, working on our experience, that puts it in our power to know, whether the painter has fixed upon the attitudes and airs in nature appropriated to the passions, characters, and actions which he would represent; and, when these attitudes are various, whether he has chosen those which most perfectly correspond with the unity and propriety of his design. Painting being circumscribed to an instant of time, judgment alone can perceive, whether that instant is properly selected, whether the artist has pitched on that moment which comprehends the circumstances most essential to the grand event, and best allows, without a deviation from simplicity, the indication of the other requisite circumstances. It estimates the due proportion of all the figures, in dignity, elegance, and luster, and their due subordination to the principle. In fine, it is necessarily employed in that exhibition of the object to the senses which must be previous to their perception of it.

In order to approve or condemn in *poetry*, or *eloquence*, we must take into view at once, and compare, so many particulars, that none can hesitate to acknowledge the absolute necessity of a sound and vigorous judgment. We must determine, whether the fable or design is well imagine in congruity to the species of the poem or discourse; whether all the incidents, or arguments are natural members of it; which of them promotes its force of beauty, or which, by its want of connection, obstructs the end, or debilitates its genuine effect; what degree of relation is sufficient to introduce episodes, illustrations, or digressions, so that they may appear, not excrescences and deformities, but suitable decorations. It is *sense* which is pleased or displeased when these things are determined: but *judgment* alone can determine them, and present to sense the object of its perception. By an accurate scrutiny of the various relations of parts, judgment fixes that situation in which they promote the regular organization on which both the elegance and vigour of the whole depends. It compares characters with nature, and pronounces them either real or monstrous. It compares them with other characters, and finds them good or bad in the kind, properly or improperly marked. It compares them with themselves, and discovers whether they are consistent or inconsistent, well or ill supported; whether their peculiar decorum is preserved or violated. Truth and justness is the foundation of every beauty in sentiment; it imparts to it that solidity, without which it may dazzle a vulgar eye, but can never please one who looks beyond the first appearance: and to ascertain truth, to unmask falsehood, however artfully disguised, is the peculiar prerogative of judgment. The finest sentiments, if applied to subjects unsuitable, may not only lose their beauty, but even throw deformity upon the whole: and judgment alone perceives the fitness or unfitness of their application. This faculty arrogates also to itself, in some degree, the cognizance of style and language; and, by bringing it to the test of custom, discovers its propriety, purity, and elegance. Judgment, not satisfied with examining separate parts, combines them, and the feelings which they produce, in order to estimate the merit of the whole. It settles the relative value of different poems and discourses, of the same or various kinds, by a studious and severe comparison of the dignity of their ends, the difficulty of attaining them, the moment of their effects, the suitableness and ingenuity of the means employed.

Thus in all the operations of taste, judgment is employed; not only in presenting the subjects on which the senses exercise themselves; but also in comparing and weighing the perceptions and decrees of the senses themselves, and thence passing ultimate sentence upon the whole.

But though the reflex senses and judgment must be united, yet, in a consistence with true taste, they may be united in very different proportions. In some, the acuteness of the senses; in others, the accurateness of the senses; in others, the accuracy of the judgment, is the predominant quality. Both will determine justly: but they are guided by different lights; the former, by the perception of sense; the latter, by the conviction of the understanding. One *feels* what pleases or displeases; the other *knows* what ought to gratify or disgust. Sense has a kind of instinctive infallibility, by means of which, when it is vigorous, it can preserve from error, though judgment should not be perfect. Judgment, by contemplating the qualities that affect taste, by surveying its sentiments in their causes, often makes amends for dullness of imagination. Where *that* prevails, one's chief entertainment from works of genius lies in what he feels: where *this* is predominant, one enjoys principally the intellectual pleasure which results from discovering the causes of his feelings. This diversity in the form and constitution of taste is very observable in two of the greatest critics of antiquity. Longinus is justly characterized

> *An ardent judge, who, zealous in his trust,*
> *With warmth gives sentence.*[3]

In him the internal senses were exquisitely delicate; but his judgment, though good, was not in proportion. On this account he delivers just sentiments with rapture and enthusiasm, and by a kind of contagion, infuses them into his readers, without always explaining to them the reason of their being so affected. Aristotle, on the contrary, appears to examine his subject, perfectly cool and unaffected; he discovers no warmth of imagination, no such admiration or ecstasy as can without reflection, transport his readers into his opinion. He derives his decisions not from the liveliness of feeling, but from the depth of penetration; and seldom pronounces them without convincing us that they are just. Some degree of the same diversity may be remarked in Bouhours and Boffu among the moderns.

Reading IX[4]

'Of the Connection of Taste with Genius'

Taste may be considered either as an essential *part*, or as a necessary *attendant* of genius, according as we consider genius in a more or less extensive manner. Everyone acknowledges that they have a very near connection. It is so evident that it has almost passed into a maxim, that the ablest performers are also the best judges in every art. How

---

[3] Pope, Alexander, *An Essay on Criticism*, l. 65.
[4] Excerpted from Alexander Gerard, *Essay on Taste, Second Edition with Corrections and Additions*, Edinburgh: A. Kincaid and J. Bell, London: A. Millar, 1776. Part III, Section II, pp. 168–175.

far the maxim is just, will best appear, by briefly determining the nature and principles of genius.

The first and leading quality of genius is *invention*, which consists in a great extent and comprehensiveness of imagination, in a readiness of associating the remotest ideas that are any way related. In a man of genius, the uniting principles are so vigorous and quick, that, whenever any idea is present to the mind, they bring into view at once all others that have the least connection with it. As the magnet selects, from a quantity of matter, the ferruginous particles which happen to be scattered through it, without making an impression on other substances; so imagination, by a similar sympathy, equally inexplicable, draws out from the whole compass of nature such ideas as we have occasion for, without attending to any others; and yet presents them with as great propriety, as if all possible conceptions had been explicitly exposed to our view, and subjected to our choice.

At first, these materials may lie in a rude and indigested chaos: but when we attentively review them, the same associating power which formerly made us sensible of their connection, leads us to perceive the different degrees of that connection; by its magical force ranges them into different species, according to these degrees; disposes the most strongly related into the same member; and sets all the members in that position which it points out as the most natural. Thus, from a confused heap of materials, collected by fancy, genius, after repeated reviews and transpositions, designs a regular and well-proportioned whole.

This brightness and force of imagination throws a lustre on its effects which will forever distinguish them from the lifeless and insipid productions of inanimated industry. Diligence and acquired abilities may assist or improve genius: but a fine imagination alone can produce it. Hence is derived its inventive power in all the subjects to which it can be applied. This is possessed in common by the musician, the painter, the poet, the orator, the philosopher, and even the mathematician. In each, indeed, its form has something peculiar, arising either from the degree of extent and comprehension of fancy; or from the peculiar prevalence of some one of the associating qualities; or from the mind being, by original constitution, education, example, or study, more strongly turned to one kind than others.

A genius for the fine arts implies, not only the power of invention or design, but likewise a capacity to express its designs in apt materials. Without this, it would not only be imperfect, but would forever lie latent, undiscovered, and useless. It is chiefly the peculiar modification of this capacity which adapts a genius to one art rather than another. To a painter, the ideas assembled by fancy must give him a view of their correspondent objects, in such order and proportion as will enable him to exhibit the original to the eye, by an imitation of it figure and colour. To form a poet, they must lead the thoughts not to the corporeal forms of things but to the signs with which, by the common use of language, they are connected; so that he may employ them with propriety, force, and harmony, in exciting strong ideas of his subject.

Culture may strengthen invention; knowledge is necessary for supplying a fund from which it may collect its materials; but improvement chiefly affects the capacity of expression. Painting requires a mechanical skill, produced by exercise; music, knowledge of the power of sounds, derived from experience; poetry and eloquence, an acquaintance with all the force which can be obtained only by careful study.

Thus genius is the grand architect which not only chooses the materials, but disposes them into a regular structure. But it is not able to finish it by itself. It needs the assistance of taste, to guide and moderate its exertions. Though the different relations of the parts, in some measure, determine the form and position of each, we acquire much ampler assurance of its rectitude, when taste has reviewed and examined both the design and execution. It serves as a check on mere fancy; it interposes its judgment; and rejects many things which unassisted genius would have allowed.

The distinct provinces of genius and taste being thus marked out, it will be easy to discover how far they are connected. They must be connected in a considerable degree, since they both spring from imagination: but as it is differently exerted in each, their connection will not be perfectly accurate and uniform.

Genius is not always attended with taste precisely equal and proportioned. It is sometimes incorrect, though copious and extensive. It is sometimes bold, yet can transfuse no delicacy or grace into its productions. But it is never found where taste is altogether wanting. The same vigour of the associating principles which renders genius quick and comprehensive, must bestow such strength on the several dependent operations of fancy which generate taste, as shall make that difficulty considerably active and perceptive.[5] The genius of the greatest masters in every kind has not been more perfect than their taste. The models they have given are so finished and correct, that the general rules and precepts of the art, afterwards established by critics, are deduced from their practice, and the very same which, though uninstructed. The epos was not subjected to rules when Homer composed the Iliad. Aristotle did not write his *Art of Poetry*, till after the greatest tragic poets of antiquity had flourished. These great originals possessed not only an excellent genius, but equal taste. The vigour of their imaginations led them into unexplored tracks; and they had such light and discernment, as, without danger of error, directed their course in this untrodden wilderness. Taste, united with genius, renders the effects of the latter like to diamonds, which have as great solidity as splendour.

But taste often prevails where genius is wanting; they may judge, who cannot themselves perform. The operations that depend on the imagination, may be vigorous enough to form a high relish, though it be destitute of that brightness and extension which is necessary for a comprehensive genius. The associating principles may be strong and active within their bounds, though these bounds be narrow. And soundness and strength of judgment may be possessed without considerable genius; but must always, if joined with any degree of the internal senses, produce acuteness and

---

[5] There is in one view a still closer connection between genius and taste. A genius for the fine arts implies, at least, *sensibility* and *delicacy* of taste, as an essential part of it. By means of this, every form strikes a man of true genius so forcibly, as perfectly to enrapture and engage him, and he selects the circumstances proper for characterizing it, and impresses them upon others, with the same vivacity that he apprehends that he apprehends them himself. See this elegantly explained in *A discourse on poetical imitation*, § I.

justness of taste. This rendered Aristotle the greatest of critics, though he was not, like Longinus, *blest with a poet's fire.*

It must however be acknowledged, that genius will always throw a peculiar brightness upon taste, as it enables one, by a kind of contagion, to catch the spirit of an author, to judge with the same disposition in which he composed, and by this means to feel every beauty with a delight and transport of which a colder critic can form no idea. The fine genius of Longinus catches fire, as it were, from the mentioning of a sublime passage, and hurries him on to emulate its sublimity in his explication of it. Quintilian, by the same union of genius with taste, delivers his sentiments with the utmost elegance, and enlivens the abstractness of precept by the most beautiful and apposite figures and images.

Five

Thomas Reid (1710–1796)

Thomas Reid was born to an influential Scottish family from Strachan, Kincardineshire, Aberdeen, on 26 April 1710. His father was the Presbyterian minister of the parish of Strachan, and Reid received his early education in the parish school, and later, Aberdeen Grammar. He entered Marischal College in 1722, studying under the regent, George Turnbull. He finished his MA in 1727, and his divinity degree in 1731.

Reid entered the ministry that same year, and later served as a librarian at Marischal (a position endowed to the college by his uncle) before becoming the minister of New Machar in 1737. While many in the parish objected to his appointment, which was by patronage, Reid won them over with his hard work and personal virtues. His first publication, a 1748 article entitled 'Essay on Quantity, occasioned by reading a Treatise in which Simple and Compound Ratios are Applied to Virtue and Merit' took issue with Hutcheson's treatment of mathematics in *An Enquiry in to our Original Ideas of Beauty and Virtue*, and was published in the transactions of the Royal Society. Reid was a keen follower of developments in the field of mathematics, an interest he maintained along with all of the sciences (especially astronomy) his entire life. It is said that until he reached old age he avidly followed the new developments in science, medicine, and politics by frequently attending courses at his own university.

In 1751, Reid was elected to Professor of Moral Philosophy at King's College, Aberdeen. There, Reid was one of the founders of the Philosophical Society (The Wise Club) and it was by virtue of the conversations and associations developed there that he wrote his *Inquiry into the Human Mind upon the Principals of Common Sense*, which was published in 1764. Hugh Blair, mutual friend of both Reid and David Hume, had given Reid Hume's manuscript, and *Inquiry* was Reid's comprehensive reply to Hume's system, as well as the theory of ideas promulgated by Locke and Descartes. He and Hume later corresponded over their works. In 1763, Reid was asked to succeed Adam Smith in the Chair of Moral Philosophy at Glasgow, which he held until his retirement at age 70. During this time Reid was very active in the intellectual societies of Glasgow and Edinburgh, and over the next two decades he worked out his comprehensive and profoundly influential philosophical system, now often known as Scottish Common Sense Realism. In 1785 Reid published *Essays on the Intellectual Powers of Man*, and its companion *Essays on the Active Powers of Man* three years later. In his last decade, Reid continued to present papers and participate in debates about the current political, scientific, legal, and economic questions of his day. He died after a brief illness on 7 October 1796.

Reid's influence on his own era was wide, as was his influence on the decades following. In America in particular, his work resonated in several fields: in political philosophy, early American thinkers are marked by Common Sensism; in higher education, many of the leading lights of the first universities were either his students or in some other ways followers; in rhetorical education, as the most widely used texts were written by those in the Common Sense school; and of course, in the origination of American pragmatism, as Reid was an unmistakable influence on C.S. Peirce. In affinity with Peirce, Thomas Reid was not only a synthetic philosophical thinker, but also a scientific and mathematical one. Reid argues in Reading IX that human speech is 'the express language and picture of human thoughts; and from this picture we may often draw certain conclusions about the original', and from this induction arises his chief advancement in the philosophy of language. Language is one of the primary indicators of what is universal in the nature of man, it is therefore one of the first places to begin an inquiry into human nature and how we come to know. Our minds are also, moreover, inherently social in many of their operations. It is from this that the impulse to rhetorical instruction derives, in Reid's followers and fellow Common Sense thinkers George Campbell and Hugh Blair.

Sources

Chalmers, Robert, 'Reid, Thomas', *Biographical Dictionary of Eminent Scotsmen,* Glasgow: Blackie and Son, 1875. Online ed. National Library of Scotland.

Cuneo, Terence and Rene Van Woudenberg, 'Introduction', *Cambridge Companion to Thomas Reid,* Cambridge, 2004.

Wood, Paul, 'Reid, Thomas (1710-1796)', *Oxford Dictionary of National Biography,* Ed. H.C.G. Matthew and Brian Harrison, Oxford: Oxford University Press, 2004. Online ed., Ed. Lawrence Goldman, Oct. 2006.

READING X[1]

That every act or operation, therefore, supposes an agent, that every quality supposes a subject, are things that I do not attempt to prove, but take for granted. Every man, of common understanding discerns this immediately and cannot entertain the least doubt of it. In all languages we find certain words, which by Grammarians, are called adjectives. Such words denote attributes, and every adjective must have a substantive to which it belongs; that is, every attribute must have a subject. In all languages we find active verbs, which denote some action or operation; and it is a fundamental rule in the grammar of all languages that such a verb supposes a person; that it, in other words, that every action must have an agent. We take it therefore, as a first principles, that goodness, wisdom, and virtue, can only be in some being the is good, wise, and virtuous; that thinking supposes a being that thinks; and that every operation that we are conscious supposes an agent that operates, that we call mind.

I take it for granted that, in most operations of the mind there must be an object distinct from the operation itself. I

---

[1] Reid, Thomas, *Essays on the Intellectual and Active Powers of Man,* Dublin: L. White, 1775. Excerpted from 'Preliminary' to Chapter 2, 'Principles Taken for Granted', pp. 36-46.

cannot see, without seeing something. Too see without having any object of sight is absurd. I cannot remember, without remembering something. The thing remembered is past, while the remembrance of it is present, and therefore the operation and the object of it must be distinct things. The operations of our minds are denoted, in all languages, by active transitive verb, which from their construction in grammar require not only a person and agent but likewise an object of the operation. Thus the verb no, denotes an operation of mind. From general structure of language this verb requires a person; I know, you know, or he knows: But it requires no less a noun in the accusative case denoting the thing known; for that he knows, must know something; and to know without having any object of knowledge is an absurdity to gross to admit of reasoning.

We ought likewise to take for granted, as first principals, things wherein we find universal agreement, among the learned and unlearned in the different ages and nations of the world. A consent of ages and nations, of the learned and vulgar, ought, at least, to have great authority, unless we can show some prejudice, as universal as that consent is, which might be the cause of it. Truth is one, but error is infinite. There are many truths so obvious to the human faculties that it may expected that men should universally agree on them. And this is actually found to be the case with regard to many truths, against which we find no dissent, unless perhaps that of a few Philosophers who many justly be suspected, in such cases, to differ from the rest of mankind, through pride, obstinacy, or some favourite passion. Where there is such universal consent in things not deep not intricate, but which lie, as it were, on the surface, there is the greatest presumption that can be, that is the result of the natural human faculties; and it must have great authority with every sober mind that loves truth. *Major enim pars eo fere diferri solet quo a natura deducitur* Cicero de Off. 1.41.[2]

Perhaps it may be thought, that it is impossible to collect the opinions of all men upon any point whatsoever, and,

---

[2] The modern text of this is somewhat different: *Major enim pars eo fere diferri solet quo a natura ipsa deducitur*. It may be translated:

therefore, that this maxim can be of no use. But there are many cases wherein it is otherwise. Who can doubt, for instance, whether mankind have, in all ages, believed the existence of a material world, and that those things which they see and handle are real, and not real illusions and apparitions? Who can doubt, whether mankind is universally believed that everything that begins to exist, and every change that happens in nature, must have a cause? Who can doubt, whether mankind have been universally persuaded that there is a right and a wrong in human conduct? Something which, in certain circumstances, they ought to do, and other things they ought not to do? The universality of these opinions, and of many such that might be named, is sufficiently evident from the whole tenor of men's conduct, as far as our acquaintance reaches, and as from the records of history, in all ages and nations, that are transmitted to us.

There are other opinions that appear to be universal, from what is common in the structure of all languages, ancient and modern, polished and barbarous. Language is the express language and picture of human thoughts; and, from the picture, we may often draw very certain conclusion with regard the original. We find in all languages the same parts of speech, nouns substantive and adjective, verbs active and passive, varied according to the tenses of past, present, and future; we find adverbs, prepositions, and conjunctions. There are general rule of syntax common to all languages. This uniformity in the structure of language shows a certain degree of uniformity of those notions upon which the structure of language is grounded.

We find, in the structure of all languages, the distinction of acting, and being acted upon, the distinction of an action and agent of quality and subject, and many others of the like kind; which shows, that these distinctions are founded in the universal sense of mankind. We shall have frequent occasion to argue from the sense of mankind expressed in the structure of language; and therefore, it was proper here to take notice of the force of arguments drawn this topic.

I need hardly say, that I shall also take for granted such fact as are attested to the conviction of all sober and reasonable men, either by our senses, by memory, or by human testimony. Although some writers on this subject have disputed the authority of the sense, of memory, and of every human faculty; yet we find, that such persons, in the conduct of life, in pursuing their ends, or in avoiding dangers, paid the same regard to the authority of their senses, and other faculties, as the rest of mankind. By this, they give us just ground to doubt of their candour in their professions of scepticism.

This, indeed, has always been the fate of the few that have professed scepticism, that when they have done what they can to discredit their senses, they find themselves, after all, under the necessity of trusting to them. My Hume has been so candid as to acknowledge this; and it is no less true of those who have not shown the same candour: for I have never heard that any sceptic run his head against a post or stepped into a kennel because he did not believe his eyes.

Upon the whole, I acknowledge that we ought to be cautious, that we do not adopt opinions as first principles which are not entitled to that character. But there is surely the least danger of men's being imposed upon in this way, when such principals openly lay claim to the character, and are thereby fairly exposed to the examination of those who may dispute their authority. We do not pretend that those things that are laid down as first principles may not be examined, and we ought not to have our ears open to what may be pleaded against their being admitted as such. Let us deal with them, as an upright judge does with a witness who has a fair character. He pays a regard to the testimony of such a witness while his character is unimpeached. But if it can be shown that he is suborned, or that he is influenced by malice or partial favour, his testimony loses all its credit and is justly rejected.

READING XI[3]

There is another division of the powers of the mind, which, though it has been, ought not to be overlooked by writers on

---

[3] Reid, Thomas, *Essays on the Intellectual and Active Powers of Man*, Dublin: L. White, 1775. Excerpt is Essay I, Chapter VIII: 'Of Social Operations of the Mind', pp. 72–74.

this subject, because it has a real foundation in nature. Some operation of our minds, from their very nature, are *social*, others *solitary*.

By the first, I understand such operations as necessarily suppose an intercourse with some other intelligent being. A man may understand and will; he may apprehend, and judge, and reason, though he should know of no intelligent being in the universe besides himself. But, when he asks information, he receives it; when he hears testimony, or receives testimony of another; when he asks a favour, or accepts one; when he gives a command to his servant, or receives one from a superior: when he plights his faith in a promise or contract; these are acts of social intercourse between intelligent beings, and can have no place in solitude. They support understanding and will; but they support something more, which is neither understanding nor will; that is society with other intelligent beings. They may call this intellectual, because they can only be in intellectual beings: but they are neither simple apprehension, nor judgment, nor reasoning, nor are they any combination of these operations.

To ask a question, is as simple an operation as to judge or to reason; yet it is neither judgment, nor reasoning, nor simple apprehension, nor is it any combination of these. Testimony is neither simple apprehension, nor judgment, nor reasoning. The same is said of a promise, or of a contract. These acts of mind are perfectly understood by every man of common understanding; but when philosophers attempt to bring them within the pale of their divisions, by analysing them, they find inexplicable mysteries, and even contradictions, in them. One may see an instance of this, of many that might be mentioned, in Mr. Hume's *Enquiry concerning the principles of morals*, sect. 3, part 2. Note, near the end.

The attempts of philosophers to reduce the social operations under the common philosophical divisions, resemble very much the attempts of some Philosophers to reduce all our social affections to certain modifications of self-love. The Author of our being intended us to be social beings, and has, for that end, given us social intellectual powers, as well as social affections. Both are original parts of our constitution, and the exertions of both no less natural than the exertions of those powers that are solitary and selfish.

Our social intellectual operations, as well as our social affections, appear very early in life, before we are capable of reasoning; yet both suppose a conviction of the existence of other intelligent beings. When a child asks a question to his nurse, this act of his mind supposes not only a desire to know what he asks; it supposes likewise a conviction that the nurse is an intelligent being, to whom he can communicate his thoughts, and who can communicate her thoughts to him. How he came by this conviction so early, is a question of some importance in the knowledge of the human mind, and therefore worthy of the consideration of philosophers. But they seem to have given no attention either to this early conviction, or to those operations of the mind, which suppose it. Of this we shall have occasion to treat afterwards.

All languages are fitted to express the social as well as the solitary operations of the minds. It may indeed be affirmed, that, to express the former, is the primary and direct intention of language. A man, who had no intercourse with any other intelligent being, would never think of language. He would be as mute as the beasts of the fields; even more so, because they have some degree of social intercourse with one another, and some of them with man. When language is once learned, it may be useful even in our solitary meditations; and, by clothing our thoughts with words we may have a firmer hold on them. But this was not its first intention; and the structure of every language shows that it is not intended solely for this purpose.

In every language, a question, a command, a promise, which are social acts, can be expressed as easily as properly as judgment, which is a solitary act. The expression of the last has been honoured with a particular name; it is called proposition; it has been an object of great attention to philosophers; it has been analysed into its very elements of subject, predicate, and copula. All various modifications of these, and of propositions which are compounded of them, have been anxiously examined in many voluminous tracts. The expression of a question, of a command, or of a promise, is as capable of being analysed as a proposition is; but we do not find that this has been attempted; we have not so much as given them a name different from the operations which they express.

Why have speculative men laboured so anxiously to analyse our solitary operations, and given so little attention to the social? I know no other reason than this, that, in the divisions that have been made of the mind's operations, the social have been omitted, and thereby thrown behind the curtain.

In all languages, the second person of the verbs, the pronoun of the second person, and the vocative case in nouns, are appropriated to the expression of social purposed of the mind, and could never have had a place in language but for this purpose: Nor is it a good argument against this observation, that, by a rhetorical figure, we sometimes address persons that are absent, or even inanimated beings, in the second person. For it ought to be remembered, that all figurative ways of using words or phrases suppose a natural and literal meaning of them.

READING XII[4]

'Of Natural Language'

One of the noblest purposes of sound undoubtedly is language; without which, mankind would hardly be able to maintain any degree of improvement above the brutes. Language is commonly considered as purely an invention of man, who by nature are no less mute than the brutes, but having a superior degree of invention and reason have been able to contrive artificial signs of their thoughts and purposes and to establish them by common consent. But the origin of language deserves to be more carefully inquired into, not only as this inquiry may be of importance for the improvement of language, but as it is related to the present subject, and tends to lay open some of the first principles of

---

[4] *Inquiry into the Human Mind upon the Principles of Common Sense*, 4th Edition, London: T. Cadell in the Strand; and Edinburgh: J. Bell and W. Creech, 1785. Excerpt is Section II, 'Of Natural Language', pp. 91–98, of Chapter 4, 'Of Hearing'.

human nature. I shall therefore offer some thoughts up this subject.

By language I understand all those signs which mankind use in order to communicate to other their thoughts and intentions, their purposes and desires. And such signs may be conceived to be of two kinds: first, such as have no meaning, but what is affixed to them by compact or agree among those who use them. These are artificial signs: secondly, such as previous to all compact or agreement, have a meaning which every man understands by the principles of his nature. Language, so far as it consists of artificial signs, may be called *artificial;* so far as it consists of nature signs, I call it *natural.*

Having premised these definitions, I think it is demonstrable, that if mankind had not a natural language, they could never have invented an artificial one by their reason and ingenuity. For all artificial language supposes some compact or agreement to affix certain meaning to certain signs; therefore, there must be compacts or agreements before the use of artificial signs; but there can be no compact or agreement without signs, nor without language; and therefore there must be a natural language before any artificial language can be invented: which was to be demonstrated.

Had language in general been a human invention as much as writing or printing, we should find whole nations as mute as the brute. Indeed, even the brutes have some natural signs by which they expressed their own thoughts, affections, and desires, and understand those of others. A chick, as soon as hatched, understands the different sounds whereby its dam calls it to food, or gives the alarm of danger. A dog or a horse understands, by nature, when the human voice caresses, and when it threatens him.

But brutes, as far as we know, have no notion of contracts or covenants, or of moral obligation to perform them. If nature had given them these notions, she would probably have given them natural signs to express them. And where nature has denied these notions, it is impossible to acquire them by art, as it is for a blind man to acquire the notion of colours. Some brutes are sensible of honour or disgrace; they have resentment and gratitude; but none of them, as far as we know, can make a promise, or plight their faith, having no such notions from their constitution. And if mankind had not these notions by their nature, and natural signs to express them but with all their wit and ingenuity they could never have invented language.

The elements of this natural language of mankind, or the signs that are naturally expressive of our thought, may I think, be reduced to these three kinds: modulations of the voice, gestures, and features. By means of these, two savages, who have no common artificial language, can converse together; can communicate their thoughts in some tolerable manner; can ask and refuse, affirm and deny, threaten and supplicate; can traffic, enter into covenants, and plight their faith. This might be confirmed by historical facts of undoubted credit, if it were necessary.

Mankind having thus a common language by nature, though a scanty one, adapted only to the necessities of nature, there is no great ingenuity required in improving it by the addition of artificial signs, to supply the deficiency of the natural. These artificial signs must multiply with the arts of life and the improvements of knowledge. The articulations of the voice seem to be of all the signs, the most proper for artificial language; and as mankind have universally used them for that purpose, we may reasonably judge that nature intended them for it. But nature probably does not intend that we should lay aside the use of natural signs; it is enough that we supply their defects by artificial ones. A man that rides always in a chariot, by degrees, loses the use of his legs. And one who uses artificial signs only loses both the knowledge and the use of the natural. Mute people retain much more of the natural language than others, because necessity obliges them to use it. And for the same reason savages have much more of it than civilized nations. It is by natural signs chiefly that we give force and energy to language; and the less language has of them, it is the less expressive and persuasive. Thus, writing is less expressive than reading, and reading is less expressive than speaking without a book. Speaking without the proper and natural modulations, force, and variations of the voice, is a frigid and dead language compared with that which is attended with them. It is still more expressive when we add the language of the eyes and features; and it is then only in its perfect and natural state and attended with its proper energy, when to all of these we super-add the force of action.

Where speech is natural it will be an exercise not of the voice and lungs only, but of all the muscles of the body. Like that of mute people and savages whose language, as it has more of nature, is more expressive and is more easily learned. Is it not a pity that the refinements of a civilized life instead of supplying the defects of natural language, should root it out and plant in its stead dull and lifeless articulations of unmeaning sounds, or the scrawling of insignificant characters? The perfection of language is commonly thought to be to express human thoughts and sentiments distinctly by these dull signs; but if this is the perfection of artificial language, it is surely the corruption of the natural.

Artificial signs signify, but they do not express; they speak to the understanding, as algebraic characters do, but the passions, the affections, and the will hear them not: these continue dormant and inactive, until we speak to them in the language of nature to which they are all attention and obedience.

It were easy to show that the fine arts of the musician, the painter, the actor, and the orator, so far as they are all expressive; although the knowledge of them requires in us such a delicate taste, a nice judgment, and much study and practice; yet they are nothing else but the language of nature, which we brought into the world with us but have unlearned by disuse and so find the greatest difficulty in recovering it.

Abolish the use of articulate sounds and writing among mankind for a century and every man would be a painter, an actor, and an orator. We mean not to affirm that such an expedient is practical or if it were that the advantage would counterbalance the loss, but that as men are led by nature and necessity to converse together, they will use every mean in their power to make themselves understood. Where they cannot do this by artificial signs they will do it as far as possible by natural ones: and he that understands perfectly the use of natural signs must be the best judge in all the expressive arts.

Six

George Campbell (1719–1796)

George Campbell was born on the 25 December 1719, in Aberdeen, one of the six children of Rev. Colin Campbell and Mrs. Margaret Walker Campbell. Like Thomas Reid, he went to Aberdeen Grammar before entering Marischal College for an undergraduate in the arts curriculum. He intended to study law, as he had an older brother in the ministry, but while he was apprenticed in Edinburgh he attended the public lectures of Prof. Goldie, the Divinity Chair at Edinburgh, and also the sermons of Dr. Hugh Blair, then at Cannongate. It was at this time that he struck up a lifetime's close friendship with Blair.

When he returned to Aberdeen, upon completing his apprenticeship, he immediately entered the study of divinity, and was licensed to minister in 1746. During this period in Aberdeen, he founded the Theological Society with some of the other lights of the Aberdeen Enlightenment, including Alexander Gerard. One of the topics discussed hotly was eloquence and rhetoric. He soon after was ordained to a parish in Banchory Ternan, where he served for nine years. Because of the notable reputation he earned as a country minister, he was asked back to Aberdeen to minister to one of the quarters of the city. At this time he helped found the Philosophical Society with Thomas Reid, John Stewart, James Beattie, John Gregory, and Alexander Gerard, where he delivered many of the papers that would become his *Philosophy of Rhetoric*. In 1759, he was chosen (through family patronage of the Duke of Argyle) to become a principal of

Marichal College. He soon received his Doctorate in Divinity from King's College, and published the *Dissertation on Miracles* (1762), a popularly successful refutation of Hume's *On Miracles*. This work secured his reputation as a scholar and academic of note, and when Gerard stepped down from the Professor of Divinity in 1771, Campbell was asked to the position. During the next few years he published *The Philosophy of Rhetoric* (1776) and the later *The Four Gospels* (1789). He was also notably involved in some public theological controversies of his day regarding religious toleration. Campbell was a firm defender of political and religious toleration, which on one occasion brought protesters to his home in Aberdeen. Campbell, whose health had always been troublesome, resigned due to age and illness in 1795, at the age of seventy-six, and died a year later. After his death, his lectures were published in three volumes: *Lectures on Ecclesiastical History* (1800), *Lectures on Systematic Theology and Pulpit Eloquence* (1807), and *Lectures on the Pastoral Character* (1811).

Campbell's *Rhetoric* was reprinted 21 times in the century following his death, and it was used widely as a canonical text in the study of writing at colleges in Britain and America. It is properly, as the reader will soon see, a *philosophy* of rhetoric, in that it is a theoretical exploration of the 'critical science' of the study of the use of language. By applying a scientific method to our uses of language, we can discern 'the principals in our nature to which the various attempts are adapted, and in what circumstances only to be used' (Reading XIII), in a way that is evidential, not theoretical. Campbell's work, as a philosophy, is remarkable for its use of rhetorical examination as inductive metaphysical reasoning, as his careful delineation of scientific and moral evidence demonstrates.

Sources

Bitzer, Lloyd, 'Introduction' to Campbell, George, *Philosophy of Rhetoric*, Carbondale: Southern Illinois University Press, 1963.

Suderman, Jeffrey M., 'Campbell, George (1719–1796)', *Oxford Dictionary of National Biography*, Ed. H.C.G. Matthew and Brian Harrison, Oxford: Oxford University Press, 2004. Online ed., Ed. Lawrence Goldman, Oct. 2006.

Suderman, J.M., *Orthodoxy and Enlightenment: George Campbell in the Eighteenth Century*, Montreal: McGill-Queen's University Press, 2001.

Reading XIII[1]

Introduction to the Philosophy of Rhetoric

All art is founded in science, and the science is of little value which does not serve as a foundation to some beneficial art. On the most sublime of all sciences, *theology* and *ethics*, is built the most important of all arts, *the art of living*. The abstract mathematical sciences serve as a ground-work to the arts of the land-measurer and the accountant; and in conjunction with natural philosophy, including geography and astronomy, to those of the architect, the navigator, the dialist, and many others. Of what consequence anatomy is to surgery, and that part of physiology which teaches the laws of gravitation and of motion is to the artificer, is a matter too obvious to need illustration. The general remark might, if necessary, be exemplified throughout the whole circle of arts, both useful and elegant. Valuable knowledge, therefore, always leads to some practical skill, and is perfected in it. On the other hand, the practical skill loses much of its beauty and extensive utility, which does not originate in knowledge. There is by consequence a natural relation between the sciences and the arts, like that which subsists between the parent and the offspring.

I acknowledge indeed that these are sometimes unnaturally separated; and that by the mere influence of example on the one hand, and imitation on the other, some progress may be made in an art, without the knowledge of the principles from which it sprung. By the help of a few rules, which men are taught to use mechanically, a good practical arithmetician may be formed, who neither knows the reasons on which the rules he works by were first established, nor ever thinks it of any moment to inquire into them. In like manner, we frequently meet with expert artisans, who

---

[1] Excerpted from *The Philosophy of Rhetoric,* Edinburgh: T. Cadell and W. Davies; London: W. Strahan, 1776, 'Introduction', pp. 1–24.

are ignorant of the six mechanical powers, which, though in the exercise of their profession they daily employ, they do not understand the principles whereby, in any instance, the result of their application is ascertained. The propagation of the arts may therefore be compared more justly to that variety which takes in the vegetable kingdom, than to the uniformity which obtains universally in the animal world; for, as to the anomalous race of zoophytes, I do not comprehend them in the number. It is not always necessary that the plant spring from the seed, a slip from another plant will often answer the purpose.

There is, however, a very considerable difference in the expectations that may justly be raised from the different methods followed in the acquisition of the art. Improvements, unless in extraordinary instances of genius and sagacity, are not to be expected from those who have acquired all their dexterity from imitation and habit. One who has had an education no better than that of an ordinary mechanic, may prove an excellent manual operator; but it is only in the well instructed mechanician that you would expect to find a good mechanist. The analogy to vegetation, above suggested, holds here also. The offset is commonly no more than a mere copy of the parent plant. It is from the seed only you can expect, with the aid of proper culture, to produce new varieties, and even to make improvements on the species. 'Expert men,' says Lord Bacon, 'can execute and judge of particulars, one by one; but the general counsels, and the plots and marshalling affairs, come best from those that are learned.'

Indeed, in almost every art, even as used by mere practitioners, there are certain rules, as hath been already hinted, which must carefully be followed, and which serve the artist instead of principles. An acquaintance with these is one step, and but one step towards science. Thus in the common books of arithmetic, intended solely for practice, the rules laid down for the ordinary operations, as for numeration, or numerical notation, addition, subtraction, multiplication, division, and a few others, which are sufficient for all the superficial observer, may be thought to supersede the study of anything further. But their utility reaches a very little way, compared with that which results from the knowledge of the foundations of the art, and of what has been, not unfitly, styled *arithmetic universal*. It may be justly said that, without some portion of this knowledge, the practical rules had never been invented. Besides, if by these the particular questions which come exactly within the description of the rule may be solved; by the other, such general rules themselves, as serve for the solution of endless particulars, may be discovered.

The case I own is somewhat different with those arts which are entirely founded on experiment and observation, and are not derived, even of these, when we rise from the individual to the species, from the species to the genus, and thence to the most extensive orders and classes, we arrive, though in a different way, at the knowledge of general truths, which, in a certain sense, are also scientific, and answer a similar purpose. Our acquaintance with nature and its laws is so much extended, that we shall be enabled, in numberless cases, not only to apply to the most profitable purposes the knowledge we have thus acquired, but to determine beforehand, with sufficient certainty, the success of every new application. In this progress we are like people who, from a low and narrow bottom, where the view is confined to a few acres, gradually ascend a lofty peak or promontory. The prospect is perpetually enlarging as we mount, and when we reach the summit, the boundless horizon, comprehending all the variety of sea and land, hill and valley, town and country, arable and desert, lies under the eye at once.

Those who in medicine have scarcely risen to the discernment of any general principles, and have no other directory but the experience gained in the first and lowest stage, or as it were at the foot of the mountain, are commonly distinguished by the name of *empirics*. Something similar may be said to obtain in the other liberal arts; for in all of them more enlargement of mind is necessary than is required for the exercise of those called mechanical. The character directly opposite to the *empiric* is the *visionary*; for it is not in theology only that there are visionaries. Of the two extremes I acknowledge that the latter is the worse. The first founds upon facts, but the facts are few, and commonly in his reasonings, through his imperfect knowledge of the subject, misapplied. The second often argues very consequentially from principles which, having no foundation in nature, may justly be denominated the illegitimate issue of his own imagination. He in this resembles the man of science, that he acts systematically, for there are false as well as true theorists, and is influenced by certain general propositions, real or imaginary. But the difference lies here, that in the one they are real, in the other imaginary. The system of the one is reared on the firm basis of experience, the theory of the other is no better than a castle in the air. I mention characters only in the extreme, because in this manner they are best discriminated. In real life, however, any two of these, sometimes all the three, in various proportions, may be found blended in the same person.

The arts are frequently divided into the useful, and the polite, fine, or elegant; for these words are, in this application, used synonymously. This division is not coincident with that into the mechanical and the liberal. Physic navigation, and the art of war, though properly liberal arts, fall entirely under the denomination of the usual; whereas painting and sculpture, though requiring a good deal of manual labour, and in that respect more nearly related to the mechanical, belong to the class denominated elegant. The first division arises purely from the consideration of the end to be attained; the second from the consideration of the means to be employed. In respect of the end, an art is either useful or elegant; in respect of the means, it is either mechanical or liberal. The true foundation of the former distribution is, that certain arts are manifestly and ultimately calculated for profit or use; whilst others, on the contrary, seem to terminate in pleasing. The one supplies a real want, the other only gratifies some mental taste. Yet, in strictness, in the execution of the useful arts there is often scope for elegance, and the arts called elegant are by no means destitute of use. The principal difference is, that use is the direct and avowed purpose of the former, whereas it is more latently and indirectly affected by the latter. Under this class are commonly included, not only the arts of the painter and statuary, but those also of the musician and the poet. Eloquence and architecture, by which last term is always understood more than building merely for accommodation, are to be considered as of a mixed nature, wherein utility and beauty have almost equal influence.

The elegant arts, as well as the useful, are founded in experience, but from the difference of their nature there arises a considerable difference both in their origin and in their growth. Necessity, the mother of invention, drives men, in the earliest state of society, to the study and cultivation of the useful arts; it is always leisure and abundance which lead men to seek gratifications no way conducive to the preservation either of the individual or of the species. The elegant arts, therefore, are doubtless to be considered as the younger sisters. The progress of the former towards perfection is, however, much slower than that of the latter. Indeed, with regard to the first, it is impossible to say, as to several arts, what is the perfection of the art; since we are incapable of conceiving how far the united discernment and industry of men, properly applied, may yet carry them. For some centuries backwards, the men of every age have made great and unexpected improvements on the labours of their predecessors. And it is very probable that the subsequent age will produce discoveries and acquisitions, which we of this age are as little capable of foreseeing, as those who preceded us in the last century were capable of conjecturing the progress that would be made in the present. The case is not entirely similar in the fine arts. These, though later in their appearing, are more rapid in their advancement. There may, indeed, be in these a degree of perfection beyond what we have experienced; but we have some conception of the very utmost to which it can proceed. For instance, where resemblance is the object, as in a picture or statue, a perfect conformity to its archetype is a thing at least conceivable. In like manner, the utmost pleasure of which the imagination is susceptible, by a poetical narrative or exhibition, is a thing, in my judgment, not inconceivable. We Britons, for example, do, by immense degrees, excel the ancient Greeks in the arts of navigation and ship-building; and how much further we may still excel them in these, by means of discoveries and improvements yet to be made, it would be the greatest presumption in any man to say. But as it requires not a prophetic spirit to discover, it implies no presumption to affirm, that we shall never excel them so far in poetry and eloquence, if ever in these respects we come to equal them. The same thing might probably be affirmed in regard to painting, sculpture, and music, if we had here as ample a fund of materials for forming a comparison.

But let it be observed, that the remarks now made regard only the advancement of the arts themselves; for though the useful are of slower growth than the other, and their utmost perfection cannot always be so easily ascertained, yet the acquisition of any one of them by a learner in the perfection which it has reached at the time, is a much easier matter than the acquisition of any of the elegant arts;—besides that the latter require much more of a certain happy combination in the original frame of spirit, commonly called genius, than is necessary to the other.

Let it be observed further, that as the gratification of taste is the immediate object of the fine arts, their effect is in a manner instantaneous, and the quality of any new production in these is immediately judged by everybody; for all have in them some rudiments of taste, though in some they are improved by a good; in others corrupted by a bad education, and in others almost suppressed by a total want of education. In the useful arts, on the contrary, as more time and experience are requisite for discovering the means by which our accommodation is effected, so it generally requires examination, time, and trial, that we may be satisfied of the fitness of the work for the end proposed. In these we are not near so apt to consider ourselves as judges, unless we be either artists, or accustomed to employ and examine the work of artists in that particular profession.

I mentioned some arts that have their fundamental principles in the abstract sciences of geometry and arithmetic, and some in the doctrine of gravitation and motion. There are others, as the medical and chirurgical arts,[2] which require a still broader foundation of science and anatomy, the animal economy, natural history, diseases, and remedies. Those arts which, like poetry, are purely to be ranked among the elegant, as their end is attained by an accommodation to some

---

[2] Surgical.

internal taste, so the springs by which alone they can be regulated must be sought for in the nature of the human mind, and more especially in the principles of the imagination. It is also in the human mind that we must investigate the source of some of the useful arts. Logic, whose end is the discovery of truth, is founded in the doctrine of the understanding, and ethics (under which may be comprehended economics, politics, and jurisprudence) are founded in that of the will.

This was the idea of Lord Verulam,[3] perhaps the most comprehensive genius in philosophy that has appeared in modern times. But these are not the only arts which have their foundation in the science of human nature. Grammar too, in its general principles, has a close connection with the understanding, and the theory of the association of ideas.

But there is no art whatever that hath so close a connection with all the faculties and powers of the mind, as eloquence, or the art of speaking, in the extensive sense in which I employ the term. For in the first place, that it ought to be ranked among the polite or fine arts, is manifest from this, that in all its exertions, with little or no exception, (as

---

[3] Doctrina circa *intellectum,* atque illa altera circa *voluntatem* hominis, in natalibus suis tanquam gemelae sunt. Etenim illuninationis *puritas* et *arbitrii libertas* simul inceperunt, simul corruerunt. Neque datur in universitate rerum tam intima sympathia quam illa *Veri* et *Boni.* — Venimus jam ad doctrinam circa usum et objecta facultatum animae humanae. Illa duas habet partes easque notissimas, et consensu receptas, *Logicam* et *Ethicam.* — Logica de intellectu et ratione: Ethica de voluntate, appetitu, et affectibus disserit. Altera decreta, altera actiones progignit. De Aug. Sci.l. v., c. 1. [Francis Bacon, *De Augmentis Scientiarum.*]

[The doctrine concerning intellect, and also the other about the human will, in their births are as twins. For indeed the purity of illumination and the liberty of judgment begin and end together. Nor is it given in the universe of things so intimate a sympathy as that of Truth and Good. We have come now to the doctrine around the use and object of the faculties of the human 'anima'. That anima has two parts and these are most notable, and received in consensus, Logic and Ethics. Logic treats of intellect and reason: Ethics will, appetite, and feelings. The former gives rise to resolve, the latter to actions. — Bacon.]

will appear afterwards,) it requires the aid of the imagination. Thereby it not only pleases, but by pleasing commands attention, rouses the passions, and often at last subdues the most stubborn resolution. It is also a useful art. This is certainly the case if the power of speech be a useful faculty, as it professedly teaches us how to employ that faculty with the greatest probability of success. Further, if the logical art, and the ethical, be useful, eloquence is useful, as it instructs us how these arts must be applied for the conviction and the persuasion of others. It is indeed the grand art of communication, not of ideas only, but of sentiments, passions, dispositions, and purposes. Nay, without this, the greatest talents, even wisdom itself, lose much of their lustre, and still more of their usefulness. 'The wise in heart,' saith Solomon, 'shall be called prudent, but the sweetness of the lips increaseth learning' (Proverbs xvi.21). By the former a man's own conduct may be well regulated, but the latter is absolutely necessary for diffusing valuable knowledge, and enforcing right rules of action upon others.

Poetry indeed is properly no other than a particular mode or form of certain branches of oratory. But of this more afterwards. Suffice it only to remark at present, that the direct end of the former, whether to delight the fancy as in epic, or to move the passions as in tragedy, is avowedly in part the aim, and sometimes the immediate and proposed aim, of the orator. The same medium, language, is made use of; the same general rules of composition, in narration, description, argumentation, are observed; and the same tropes and figures, either for beautifying or for invigorating the diction, are employed by both. In regard to versification, it is more to be considered as an appendage, than as a constituent of poetry. In this lies what may be called the more mechanical part of the poet's work, being at most but a sort of garnishing, and by far too unessential to give a designation to the kind. This particularity in form, to adopt an expression of the naturalists, constitutes only variety, and not a different species.

Now, though a considerable proficiency in the practice of the oratorical art may be easily and almost naturally attained by one in whom clearness of apprehension is happily united with sensibility of taste, fertility of imagination, and a certain readiness in language; a more thorough investigation of the latent energies, if I may thus express myself, whereby the instruments employed by eloquence produce their effect upon the hearers, will serve considerably both to improve the taste, and to enrich the fancy. By the former effect we learn to amend and avoid faults in composing and speaking, against which the best natural but uncultivated parts give no security; and by the latter, the proper mediums are suggested, whereby the necessary aids of topics, arguments, illustrations, and motives, may be procured. Besides, this study, properly conducted, leads directly to an acquaintance with ourselves; it not only traces the operations of the intellect and imagination, but discloses the lurking springs of action in the heart. In this view it is perhaps the surest and the shortest, as well as the pleasantest way of arriving at the science of the human mind. It is a humble attempt to lead the mind of the studious inquirer into this tract, that the following sheets are now submitted to the examination of the public.

When we consider the manner in which the rhetorical art hath arisen, and been treated in the schools, we must be sensible that in this, as in the imitative arts, the first handle has been given to criticism by actual performances in the art. The principles of our nature will, without the aid of any previous and formal instruction, sufficiently account, for the first attempts. As speakers existed before grammarians, and reasoners before logicians, so doubtless there were orators before there were rhetoricians, and poets before critics. The first impulse towards the attainment of every art is Nature. The earliest assistance and direction that can be obtained in the rhetorical art, by which men operate on the minds of others, arises from the consciousness a man has of what operates on his own mind, aided by the sympathetic feelings, and by that practical experience of mankind, which individuals, even in the rudest state of society, are capable of acquiring. The next step is to observe and discriminate by proper appellations, whether modes of arguing, or forms of speech, that have been employed for the purposes of explaining, convincing, pleasing, moving, and persuading. Here we have the beginnings of the critical science. The third step is to compare, with diligence, the various effects, favourable or unfavourable, of those attempts, carefully taking into consideration every attendant circumstance by which the success appears to have been influenced, and by which one may be enabled to discover to what particular purpose each attempt is adapted, and in what circumstances only to be used. The fourth and last is to canvass those principles in our nature to which the various attempts are adapted, and by which, in any instance, their success or want of success may be accounted for. By the first step the critic is supplied with materials. By the second, the materials are distributed and classed, the forms of argument, the tropes and figures of speech, with their divisions and subdivisions, are explained. By the third, the rules of composition are discovered, or the method of combining and disposing the several materials, so as that they may be perfectly adapted to the end in view. By the fourth, we arrive at that knowledge of human nature which, besides its other advantages, adds both weight and evidence to all precedent discoveries and rules.

The second of the steps above mentioned, which, by the way, is the first of the rhetorical art, for all that precedes is properly supplied by Nature, appeared to the author of Hudibris the utmost pitch that had even to his time been attained:

For all a rhetorician's rules, Teach nothing but to *name* his tools.[4]

In this, however, the matter has been exaggerated by the satirist. Considerable progress had been made by the ancient Greeks and Romans, in devising the proper rules of composition, not only the two sorts of poesy, epic and dramatic, but also in the three sorts of orations which were in most frequent use among them, the deliberative, the judiciary, and the demonstrative. And I must acknowledge that, as far as I have been able to discover, there has been little or no improvement in this respect made by the moderns. The observations and rules transmitted to us from these distinguished names in the learned world, Aristotle, Cicero, and

---

[4] Samuel Butler (1612–1680), 'Hudibras', part 1, Canto 1, line 75.

Quintilian, have been for the most part only translated by later critics, or put into a modish dress and new arrangement. And as to the fourth and last step, it may be said to bring us into a new country, of which, though there have been some successful incursions occasionally made upon its frontiers, we are not yet in full possession.

The performance which, of all those I happen to be acquainted with, seems to have advanced farthest in this way, is the *Elements of Criticism*. But the subject of the learned and ingenious author of that work is rather too multifarious to admit so narrow a scrutiny as would be necessary for a perfect knowledge of the several parts. Everything that is an object of taste, *sculpture, painting, music, architecture,* and *gardening,* as well as *poetry* and *eloquence,* come within his plan. On the other hand, though his subject be more multiform, it is, in respect of its connection with the mind, less extensive than that here proposed. All those particular arts are examined only on that side wherein there is found pretty considerable coincidence with one another; namely, as objects of taste, which, by exciting sentiments of grandeur, beauty, novelty, and the like, are calculated to delight the imagination. In this view, eloquence comes no further under consideration, than as a fine art, and adapted, like the others above mentioned, to please the fancy, and to move the passions. But to treat it also as a useful art, and closely connected with the understanding and the will would have led to a discussion foreign to his purpose.

I am aware that, from the deduction given above, it may be urged, that the fact, as here represented, seems to subvert the principle formerly laid down, and that as practice in the art has given the first scope for criticism, the former cannot justly be considered as deriving light and direction from the latter; that, on the contrary, the latter ought to be regarded as merely affording a sort of intellectual entertainment to speculative men. It may be said that this science, however entertaining, as it must derive all its light and information from the actual examples in the art, can never in return be subservient to the art, from which alone it has received whatever it has to bestow. This objection, however specious, will not bear a near examination. For let it be observed, that though in all the arts the first rough drafts, or imperfect attempts, that are made, precede everything that can be termed criticism, they do not precede everything that can be termed, knowledge, which every human creature that is not an idiot, is every day from his birth acquiring by experience and observation. This knowledge must of necessity precede *even* those rudest and earliest essays; and if; in the imperfect and indigested state in which knowledge must always be found in the mind that is rather self-taught than totally untaught, it deserves not to be dignified with the title of Science, neither does the first awkward attempt in practice merit to be honoured with the name of Art. As is the one, such is the other. It is enough for my purpose that something must be known, before anything in this way, with a view to an end, can be undertaken to be done.

At the same time it is acknowledged, that as man is much more an active than a contemplative being, and as generally there is some view to action, especially in uncultivated minds, in all their observations and inquiries, it cannot be doubted that, in composition, the first attempts would be in the art, and that afterwards, from the comparison of different attempts with one another, and the consideration of the success with which they had been severally attended, would arise gradually the rules of criticism. Nor can it, on the other hand, be pleaded with any appearance of truth, that observations derived from the productions of an art can be of no service for the improvement of that art, and consequently of no benefit to future artists. On the contrary, it is thus that every art, liberal or mechanical, elegant or useful, except those founded in pure mathematics, advances towards perfection. From observing similar but different attempts and experiments, and from comparing their effects, general remarks are made, which serve as so many rules for directing future practice; and from comparing such general remarks together, others still more general are deduced. A few individual instances serve as a foundation to those observations, which, when once sufficiently established, extend their influence to instances innumerable. It is in this way that, on experiments comparatively few, all the physiological sciences have been reared; it is in this way that those comprehensive truths were first discovered, which have had such an unlimited influence on the most important arts, and given man so vast a dominion over the elements, and even the most refractory powers of nature. It is evident, therefore, that the artist and the critic are reciprocally subservient, and the particular province of each is greatly improved by the assistance of the other.

But it is not necessary here to *enter* further into this subject; what I shalt have occasion afterwards to advance on the acquisition of experience, and the manner of using it, will be a sufficient illustration.

READING XIV[5]

'The Nature and Foundations of Eloquence'

In speaking there is always some end proposed, or some effect which the speaker intends to produce on the hearer. The word *eloquence* in its greatest latitude denotes, 'That art or talent by which the discourse is adapted to its end.'[6]

All the ends of speaking are reducible to four; every speech being intended to enlighten the understanding, to please the imagination, to move the passions, or to influence the will.

Any one discourse admits only one of these ends as the principal. Nevertheless, in discoursing on a subject, many things may be introduced, which are more immediately and apparently directed to some of the other ends of speaking,

---

[5] Excerpted from *The Philosophy of Rhetoric*, Edinburgh: T. Cadell and W. Davies; London: W. Strahan, 1776, Book I, Chapter 1, 'Eloquence in the largest acceptation defined, its more general forms exhibited, with their different Objects, Ends, and Characters', pp. 25–40.

[6] Campbell's footnote: 'Dicere secundum virtutem orationis. Seientia bone dicendi.' – Quintilian. [Speaking is the second virtue of eloquence. Understanding of speaking well is the first. – Quintilian.] The word *eloquence*, in common conversation, is seldom used in such a comprehensive sense. I have, however, made choice of this definition on a double account: 1st. It exactly corresponds to Tully's idea of a perfect orator; 'Optimus est orator qui dicendo animas audientium et docet, et delectat, et permovet.' [The best orator is one who with his speaking instructs the minds of the listeners, and both delights them and moves them. – Cicero.] 2dly. It is best adapted to the subject of these papers.

and not to that which is the chief intent of the whole. But then these other and immediate ends are in effect but means, and must be rendered conducive to that which is the primary intention. Accordingly, the propriety or the impropriety of the introduction of such secondary ends, will always be inferred from their subserviency or want of subserviency to that end, which is, in respect of them, the ultimate. For example, a discourse addressed to the understanding, and calculated to illustrate or evince some point purely speculative, may borrow *aid* from the imagination, and admit metaphor and comparison, but not the bolder and more striking figures, as that called vision or fiction,[7] prosopopoeia, and the like, which are not so much intended to elucidate a subject, as to excite admiration. Still less will it admit an address to the passions, which, as it never fails to disturb the operation of the intellectual faculty, must be regarded by every intelligent hearer as foreign at least, if not insidious. It is obvious, that either of these, far from being subservient to the main design, would distract the attention from it.

There is indeed one kind of address to the understanding, and only one, which, it may not be improper to observe, disdains all assistance whatever from the fancy. The address I mean is mathematical demonstration. As this does not, like moral reasoning, admit degrees of evidence, its perfection, in point of eloquence, if so uncommon an application of the term may be allowed, consists in perspicuity. Perspicuity here results entirely from propriety and simplicity of diction, and from accuracy of method, where the mind is regularly, step by step, conducted forwards in the same track, the

---

[7] Campbell's footnote: By vision or fiction is understood, that rhetorical figure of which Quintilian says, 'Quas *phantasia* Graeci vocant, nos sane visions appellamus, per quas imagines rerum absentium ita repreasantur animo, u teas cernere oculis as praesentes habere videamur.' [That which the Greeks call 'phantasies', we sensibly name 'visions', through which images of absent things are so represented to the mind that we seem to discern them with our eyes and have them present. —Quintilian.] [*Phantasia,* used in the Greek in the way Quintilian does, is a rhetorical term for imagery — to represent something using the representative and presentative faculty of imagination.]

attention no way diverted, nothing left to be supplied, no one unnecessary word or idea introduced.[8] On the contrary, a harangue framed for affecting the hearts or influencing the resolves of an assembly needs greatly the assistance both of intellect and of imagination.

In general it may be asserted, that each preceding species, in the order above exhibited, is preparatory to the subsequent, that each subsequent species is founded on the preceding, and that thus they ascend in a regular progression. Knowledge, the object of the intellect, furnishes materials for the fancy. The fancy culls, compounds, and, by her mimic art, disposes these materials so as to affect the passions. The passions are the natural spurs to volition or action, and so need only to be right directed. This connection and dependency will better appear from the following observations.

When a speaker addresses himself to the understanding, he proposes the *instruction* of his hearers, and that, either by explaining some doctrine unknown, or not distinctly comprehended by them, or by proving some position disbelieved or doubted by them. In other words, he proposes either to dispel ignorance or to vanquish error. In the one, his aim is their *information;* in the other, their *conviction.* Accordingly the predominant quality of the former is *perspicuity;* of the latter, *argument.* By that we are made to know, by this to believe.

The imagination is addressed by exhibiting to it a lively and beautiful representation of a suitable object. As in this exhibition, the task of the orator may, in some sort, be said, like that of the painter, to consist in imitation, the merit of the work results entirely from these two sources; dignity, as well in the subject or thing imitated, as in the manner of imitation; and resemblance, in the portrait or performance. Now the

---

[8] Campbell's footnote: Of this kind Euclid hath given us the most perfect models, which have not, I think, been sufficiently imitated by later mathematicians. In him you find the exactest arrangement inviolably observed, the properest and simplest, and by consequence the plainest expressions constantly used, nothing deficient, nothing superfluous; in brief, nothing which in more, or fewer, or other words, or words otherwise disposed, could have been better expressed.

principal scope for this class being in narration and description, poetry, which is one mode of oratory, especially epic poetry, must be ranked under it. The effect of the dramatic, at least of tragedy, being upon the passions, the drama falls under another species, to be explained afterwards. But that kind of address of which I am now treating, attains the summit of perfection in the *sublime*, or those great and noble images, which, when in suitable colouring presented to the mind, do, as it were, distend the imagination with some vast conception, and quite ravish the soul.

The sublime, it may be urged, as it raiseth admiration, should be considered as one species of address to the passions. But this objection, when examined, will appear superficial. There are few words in any language (particularly such as relate to the operations and feelings of the mind) which are strictly univocal. Thus admiration, when persons are the object, is commonly used for a high degree of esteem; but when otherwise applied, it denotes solely an internal taste. It is that pleasurable sensation which instantly arises on the perception of magnitude, or of whatever is great and stupendous in its kind. For there is a greatness in the degrees of quality in spiritual subjects, analogous to that which subsists in the degrees of quantity in material things. Accordingly, in all tongues, perhaps without exception, the ordinary terms, which are considered as literally expressive of the latter, are also used promiscuously to denote the former. Now admiration, when thus applied, doth not require to its production, as the passions generally do, any reflex view of motives or tendencies, or of any relation either to private interest, or to the good of others; and ought therefore to be numbered among those original feelings of the mind, which are denominated by some the reflex senses, being of the same class with a taste for beauty, an ear for music, or our moral sentiments. Now, the immediate view of whatever is directed to the imagination (whether the subject be things inanimate or animal forms, whether characters, actions, incidents, or manner, terminates in the gratification of some internal taste: as a taste for the wonderful, the fair, the good; for elegance, for novelty, or for grandeur.

But it is evident, that this creative faculty, the fancy, frequently lends her aid in promoting still nobler ends. From her exuberant stores most of those tropes and figures are extracted, which, when properly employed, have such a marvellous efficacy in rousing the passions, and by some secret, sudden, and inexplicable association, awakening all the tenderest emotions of the heart. In this case, the address of the orator is not ultimately intended to astonish by the loftiness of his images, or to delight by the beauteous resemblance which his painting bears to nature; nay, it will not permit the hearers even a moment's leisure for making the comparison, but as it were by some magical spell, hurries them, ere they are aware, into love, pity, grief, terror, desire, aversion, fury, or hatred. It therefore assumes the denomination of *pathetic*,[9] which is the characteristic of the third species of discourse, that addressed to the passions.

Finally, as that kind, the most complex of all, which is calculated to influence the will, and persuade to a certain conduct, is in reality an artful mixture of that which proposes to convince the judgment, and that which interests the passions, its distinguished excellency results from these two, the argumentative and the pathetic incorporated together. These acting with united force, and, if I may so express myself, in concert, constitute that passionate eviction, that *vehemence* of contention, which is admirably fitted for persuasion, and hath always been regarded as the supreme qualification in an orator.[10] It is this which bears down every

---

[9] Campbell's footnote: I am sensible that this word is commonly used in a more limited sense, for that which only excites commiseration. Perhaps the word impassioned would answer better.

[10] Campbell's footnote: This animated reasoning the Greek rhetoricians termed *deinotes* [meaning 'terrible', 'vehemence', 'intensity', etc.], which from signifying the principal excellency in an orator, came at length to denote oratory itself. And as vehemence and eloquence became synonymous, the latter, suitably to this way of thinking, was sometimes defined the art of persuasion. But that this definition is defective, appears even from their own writings, since in a consistency with it, their rhetorics could not have comprehended those orations called demonstrative, the design of which was not to persuade but to please. Yet it is easy to discover the origin of this defect, and that both from the nature of the thing, and from the customs which obtained among both Greeks and Romans. First, from the nature of the thing, for to persuade presupposes in some degree, and

obstacle, and procures the speaker an irresistible power over the thoughts and purposes of his audience. It is this which hath been so justly celebrated as giving one man an ascendant over others, superior even to what despotism itself can bestow; since by the latter the more ignoble part only, the body and its members are enslaved; whereas from the dominion of the former, nothing is exempted, neither judgment nor affection, not even the inmost recesses, the most latent movements of the soul. What opposition is he not prepared to conquer, on whose arms reason hath conferred solidity and weight, and passion such a sharpness as enables them, in defiance of every obstruction, to open a speedy passage to the heart?

It is not, however, every kind of pathos, which will give the orator so great an ascendancy over the minds of his hearers. All passions are not alike capable of producing this effect. Some are naturally inert and torpid; they deject the mind, and indispose it for enterprise. Of this kind are sorrow, fear, shame, humility. Others, on the contrary, elevate the soul, and stimulate to action. Such are hope, patriotism, ambition, emulation, anger. These, with the great-

---

therefore may be understood to imply, all the other talents of an orator: to enlighten, to evince, to paint, to astonish, to inflame. But this doth not hold inversely: one may explain with clearness, and prove with energy, who is incapable of the sublime, the pathetic, and the vehement. Besides, this power of persuasion, or, as Cicero calls it, '*Posse voluntates hominum impellere quo velis, undo velis, deduono*', as it makes a man master of his hearers, is the most considerable in respect of consequences. Secondly, from ancient customs. All their public orations were ranked under three classes, the demonstrative, the judiciary, and the deliberative. In the two last it was impossible to rise to eminence, without that important talent, the power of persuasion. These were in much more frequent use than the first, and withal the surest means of advancing both the fortune and the fame of the orator; for as on the judiciary the lives and estates of private persons depended, on the deliberative hung the resolves of senates, the fate of kingdoms, nay, of the most renowned republics the world ever knew. Consequently, to excel in these, must have been the direct road to riches, honours, and preferment. No wonder, then, that persuasion should almost wholly engross the rhetorician's notice.

est facility, are made to concur in direction with arguments exciting to resolution and activity: and are, consequently, the fittest for producing, what for want of a better term in our language, I shall henceforth denominate the *vehement*. There is, besides, an intermediate kind of passions, which do not so congenially and directly either restrain us from acting, or incite us to act; but, by the art of the speaker, can, in an oblique manner, be made conducive to either. Such are joy, love, esteem, compassion. Nevertheless, all these kinds may find a place in suasory discourses, or such as are intended to operate on the will. The first is properest for dissuading; the second, as hath been already hinted, for persuading; the third is equally accommodated to both.

Guided by the above reflections, we may easily trace that connection in the various forms of eloquence, which was remarked on, distinguishing them by their several objects. The imagination is charmed by a finished picture, wherein even drapery and ornament are not neglected; for here the end is pleasure. Would we penetrate further, and agitate the soul, we must exhibit only some vivid strokes, some expressive features, not decorated as for show (all ostentation being both despicable and hurtful here), but such as appear the natural exposition of those bright and deep impressions, made by the subject upon the speaker's mind; for here the end is not pleasure, but emotion. Would we not only touch the heart, but win it entirely to co-operate with our views, those affecting lineaments must be so interwoven with our argument, as that, from the passion excited our reasoning may derive importance, and so be fitted for commanding attention; and by the justness of the reasoning the passion may be more deeply rooted and enforced; and that thus both may be made to conspire in effectuating that persuasion which is the end proposed. For here, if I may adopt the schoolmen's language, we do not argue to gain barely the assent of the understanding, but, which is infinitely more important, the consent of the will.[11]

---

[11] Campbell's footnote: This subordination is beautifully and concisely expressed by Hersan in Rollin, 'Je conclus que la veritable eloquence est celle qui persuade; qu'elle ne persuade ordinairement qu'en

To prevent mistakes, it will not be beside my purpose further to remark, that several of the terms above explained are sometimes used by rhetoricians and critics in a much larger and more vague signification, than has been given them here. Sublimity and vehemence, in particular, are often confounded, the latter being considered as a species of the former. In this manner has this subject been treated by that great master Longinus, whose acceptation of the term *sublime* is extremely indefinite, importing an eminent degree of almost any excellence of speech, of whatever kind. Doubtless, if things themselves be understood, it does not seem material what names are assigned them. Yet it is both more accurate, and proves no inconsiderable aid to the right understanding of things, to discriminate by different signs such as are truly different. And that the two qualities above mentioned are of this number is undeniable, since we can produce passages full of vehemence, wherein no image is presented, which, with any propriety, can be termed great or sublime.[12] In matters of criticism, as in the abstract sciences, it

---

touchant; qu'clle no touche que par des choses at par des idées palpables.'

[12] Campbell's footnote: For an instance of this, let that of Cicero against Antony suffice. 'Tu istis faucibus istis lateribus, ista gladiatoria totius corporis firmitate, tantum vini in Hippi: nuptiis exhauseras, ut tibi necesse esset in populi Romani conspectu vomere postridie. O rem non modo visu foedam, sed etiam auditu! Si hoc tibi inter eoenam, in tuis immanibus illis poculis accidisset, quis non turpe duceret? In coetu vero populi Romani, negotium publicum gerens, magister equitum, cui ructare turpe esset, is vomens, frustis esculentis vinum redolentibus gremium suum et totum tribunal implevit.' [You with those jaws, those sides, that gladiatorial strength of your whole body, had drained so much wine at the nuptials of Hippias, that it was necessary for you the next day to vomit in the sight of the Roman people. O what a foul thing not only to see, but even to hear! If this had happened to you among that scum, in those huge cups of yours, who would not reckon it a disgrace? In the assembly of the Roman People, conducting public business, a Master of the Horse, for whom it would be a disgrace to belch, he vomiting, with edible morsels smelling of wine, filled his own lap and the whole platform.] Here the vivacity of the address, in turning from the audience to the person declaimed against, the energy of the expressions, the repetition, exclamation, interrogation, and climax of

is of the utmost consequence to ascertain, with precision, the meanings of words, and, as nearly as the genius of the language in which one writes will permit, to make them correspond to the boundaries assigned by Nature to the things signified. That the lofty and the vehement, though still distinguishable, are sometimes combined, and act with united force, is not to be denied. It is then only that the orator can be said to fight with weapons which are at once sharp, massive, and refulgent, which, like heaven's artillery, dazzle while they strike which overpower the sight and the heart at the same instant. How admirably do the two forenamed qualities, when happily blended, correspond in the rational, to the thunder and lightning in the natural world, which are not more awfully majestical in sound and aspect, than irresistible in power.[13]

---

aggravating circumstances, accumulated with rapidity upon one another, display in the strongest light the turpitude of the action, and thus at once convince the judgment and fire the indignation. It is therefore justly styled vehement. But what is the image it presents? The reverse in every respect of the sublime; what, instead of gazing on with admiration, we should avert our eyes from with abhorrence. For, however it might pass in a Roman senate, I question whether Ciceronian eloquence itself could excuse the uttering of such things in any modern assembly, not to say a polite one. With vernacular expressions, answering to these, 'vomere, ructare, frustis esculentis vinum redolentibus' [to vomit, to belch, with edible morsels smelling of wine], our more delicate ears would be immoderately shocked. In a case of this kind the more lively the picture is, so much the more abominable it is.

[13] A noted passage in Cicero's oration for Cornelius Balbus will serve as an example of the union of sublimity with vehemence. Speaking of Pompey, who had rewarded the valour and public services of our orator's client, by making him a Roman citizen, he says, 'Utrum enim inscientem vultis contra foedera fecisse, an scientem? Si scientem, O nomen nostri imperii, O populi Romani excellens dignitas, O Cneii Pompeii sic late longeque diffusa laus, ut ejus glori domicilium communis imperii finibus terminetur: O nationes, urbes, populi, reges, tetrarchae, tyranni, testes Cneii Pompeii non solum virtutis in bello, sed etiam religionis in pace: vos denique mutes regiones imploro, et sola terrarum ultimarum, vos maria, portus, insul, littoraque; qu est enim ora, qui sedes, qui locus, in quo non extent hujus cum fortitudinis, tum vero humanitatis,tum animi, tum consilii, impressa vestigia! Hunc quis quam incredibili quâdam

Thus much shall suffice for explaining the spirit, the intent, and the distinguishing qualities of each of the fore-

---

atque inauditâ gravitate, virtute, constantiâ priditum foedera scientem neglexisse, viollâsse, rupisse, dicere audebit?' [For do you wish that he had acted contrary to the treaties unknowingly or knowingly? If knowingly, O name of our empire, O excellent dignity of the Roman People, O praise of Gnaius Pompeius spread so far and wide, that the home of his universal glory is limited by the borders of the empire: O nations, cities, peoples, kings, tetrarchs, tyrants, witnesses not only of Gnaius Pompeius' courage in war, but also of his propriety in peace: further, you mute regions, I implore, and lands of the furthest countries, you seas, ports, islands, shores; for what coast, what capital, what place, is there in which the tracks of both the fortitude and the humanity of this man, of both the spirit, and of the deliberation are not stamped. Is there anybody who will dare to say that this man endowed with a certain incredible and unheard of gravitas, courage, constancy, and knowing the treaties, has neglected, violated, or broken them?] Here everything conspires to aggrandize the hero, and exalt him to something more than mortal in the minds of the auditory; at the same time, everything inspires the most perfect veneration for his character, and the most entire confidence in his integrity and judgment. The whole world is exhibited as no more than a sufficient theatre for such a superior genius to act upon. How noble is the idea! All the nations and potentates of the earth are, in a manner, produced as witnesses of his valour and his truth. Thus the orator at once fills the imagination with the immensity of the object, kindles in the breast an ardour of affection and gratitude, and, by so many accumulated evidences, convinces the understanding, and silences every doubt. Accordingly, the effect which the words above quoted, and some other things advanced in relation to the same personage, had upon the audience, as we learn from Quintilian, was quite extraordinary. They extorted from them such demonstrations of their applause and admiration, as he acknowledges to have been but ill-suited to the place and the occasion. He excuses it, however, because he considers it, not as a voluntary, but as a necessary consequence of the impression made upon the minds of the people. His words are remarkable, 'Atque ego illos credo qui aderant, nee sensisse quid facerent, nec sponte judicioque plausisse; sed velut mente captos, et quo essent in loco ignaros, erupisse in hunc voluntatis affectum' [And I also believe that those who were present, neither sensed what they were doing, nor willingly and discerningly applauded; but like those captured in mind and not knowing in what place they were, burst out into this passion of goodwill], lib. viii. cap.

mentioned sorts of address; all of which agree in this, an accommodation to affairs of a serious and important nature.

Reading XV[14]

'Of the Relation which Eloquence bears to Logic and to Grammar'

In contemplating a human creature, the most natural division of the subject is the common division into soul and body, or into the living principle of perception and of action, and that system of material organs by which the other receives information from without, and is enabled to exert its powers, both for its own benefit and for that of the species. Analogous to this, there are two things in every discourse which principally claim our attention, the sense and the expression; or in other words, the thought and the symbol by which it is communicated. These may be said to constitute the soul and the body of an oration, or indeed of whatever is signified to another by language. For, as in man, each of these constituent parts hath its distinctive attributes, and as the perfection of the latter consisteth in its fitness for serving the purposes of the former, so it is precisely with those two essential parts of every speech, the sense and the expression. Now, it is by the sense that rhetoric holds of logic, and by the expression that she holds of grammar.

The sole and ultimate end of logic is the eviction of truth; one important end of eloquence, though, as appears from the first chapter, neither the sole, nor always the ultimate, is the conviction of the hearers. Pure logic regards only the subject, which is examined solely for the sake of information. Truth, as such, is the proper aim of the examiner. Eloquence not only considers the subject, but also the speaker and the hearers, and both the subject and the speaker for the sake of the hearers, or rather for the sake of the effect intended to be produced in them. Now, to convince the hearers is always either proposed by the orator, as his end in addressing them,

---

[14] Excerpted from *The Philosophy of Rhetoric,* Edinburgh: T. Cadell and W. Davies; London: W. Strahan, 1776, Book I, Chapter IV, 'Of the Relation which Eloquence bears to Logic and Grammar', pp. 95–102.

or supposed to accompany the accomplishment of his end. Of the five sorts of discourses above mentioned, there are only two wherein conviction is the avowed purpose. One is that addressed to the understanding, in which the speaker proposes to prove some position disbelieved or doubted by the hearers; the other is that which is calculated to influence the will, and persuade to a certain conduct; for it is by convincing the judgment that he proposes to interest the passions and fix the resolution. As to the three other kinds of discourses enumerated, which address the understanding, the imagination, and the passions, conviction, though not the end, ought ever to accompany the accomplishment of the end. It is never formally proposed as an end where there are not supposed to be previous doubts or errors to conquer. But when due attention is not paid to it, by a proper management of the subject, doubts, disbelief, and mistake will be raised by the discourse itself, where there were none before, and these will not fail to obstruct the speaker's end, whatever it be. In explanatory discourses, which are of all kinds the simplest, there is a certain precision of manner which ought to pervade the whole, and which, though not in the form of argument, is not the less satisfactory, since it carries internal evidence along with it. In harangues pathetic or panegyrical, in order that the hearers may be moved or pleased, it is of great consequence to impress them with the belief of the reality of the subject. Nay, even in those performances where truth, in regard to the individual facts related, is neither sought nor expected, as in some sorts of poetry, and in romance, truth still is an object to the mind, the general truths regarding character, manners, and incidents. When these are preserved, the piece may justly be denominated true, considered as a picture of life; though false, considered as a narrative of particular events. And even these untrue events must be counterfeits of truth, and bear its image; for in cases wherein the proposed end can be rendered consistent with unbelief, it cannot be rendered compatible with incredibility. Thus, in order to satisfy the mind, in most cases, truth, and in every case, what bears the semblance of truth, must be presented to it. This holds equally, whatever be the declared aim of the speaker. I need scarcely add that to prove a particular point is often occasionally necessary in every sort of discourse, as a subordinate end conducive to the advancement of the principal. If then it is the business of logic to evince the truth, to convince an auditory, which is the province of eloquence, is but a particular application of the logician's art. As logic therefore forges the arms which eloquence teaches us to wield, we must first have recourse to the former, that being made acquainted with the materials of which her weapons and armour are severally made, we may know their respective strength and temper, and when and how each is to be used.

Now, if it be by the sense or soul of the discourse that rhetoric holds of logic, or the art of thinking and reasoning, it is by the expression or body of the discourse that she holds of grammar, or the art of conveying our thoughts in the words of a particular language. The observation of one analogy naturally suggests another. As the soul is of heavenly extraction and the body of earthly, so the sense of the discourse ought to have its source in the invariable nature of truth and right, whereas the expression can derive its energy only from the arbitrary conventions of men, sources as unlike, or rather as widely different, as the breath of the Almighty and the dust of the earth. In every region of the globe we may soon discover, that people feel and argue in much the same manner, but the speech of one nation is quite unintelligible to another. The art of the logician is accordingly, in some sense, universal; the art of the grammarian is always particular and local. The rules of argumentation laid down by Aristotle, in his Analytics, are of as much use for the discovery of truth in Britain or China as they were in Greece; but Priscian's rules of inflection and construction can assist us in learning no language but Latin. In propriety there cannot be such a thing as a universal grammar, unless there were such a thing as a universal language. The term has sometimes, indeed, been applied to a collection of observations on the similar analogies that have been discovered in all tongues, ancient and modern, known to the authors of such collections. I do not mention this liberty in the use of the term with a view to censure it. In the application of technical or learned words, an author hath greater scope than in the application of those which are in more frequent use, and is only then thought censurable when he exposes himself to be misunderstood. But it is to my purpose to observe that, as such collections convey the knowledge of no tongue whatever, the name grammar, when applied to them, is used in a sense quite different from that which it has in the common acceptation; perhaps as different, though the subject be language, as when it is applied to a system of geography.

Now, the grammatical art has its completion in syntax; the oratorical, as far as the body or expression is concerned, in style. Syntax regards only the composition of many words into one sentence; style, at the same time that it attends to this, regards further the composition of many sentences into one discourse. Nor is this the only difference; the grammarian, with respect to what the two arts have in common — the structure of sentences, requires only purity; that is, that the words employed belong to the language, and that they be construed in the manner, and used in the signification which custom has rendered necessary for conveying the sense. The orator requires also beauty and strength. The highest aim of the former is the lowest aim of the latter: where grammar ends eloquence begins.

Thus the grammarian's department bears much the same relation to the orator's which the art of the mason bears to that of the architect. There is, however, one difference that well deserves our notice. As in architecture it is not necessary that he who designs should execute his own plans, he may be an excellent artist in this way who would handle very awkwardly the hammer and the trowel. But it is alike incumbent on the orator to design and to execute. He must, therefore, be master of the language he speaks or writes, and must be capable of adding to grammatic purity those higher qualities of elocution which will render his discourse graceful and energetic.

So much for the connection that subsists between rhetoric and these parent arts, logic and grammar.

Seven

Hugh Blair
(1718–1800)

Hugh Blair was born in Edinburgh in 1718. His father was a town magistrate, and he was educated at home until entering the Tounis Scule (High School) of Edinburgh. There he received a comprehensive Latin education (fellow graduates include David Hume and John Witherspoon, among others), in which classical rhetorical texts were a strong component. He entered the University of Edinburgh in 1730, at the tender (but not unusual) age of 13, where he took an arts undergraduate, and in, 1739, received his Master of Arts. He won some distinction during his time there for an essay that he wrote for Prof. John Stevenson 'On the Beautiful', which was read publicly at the end of the course, and indicates Blair's sustained interest in aesthetic inquiry. He was licensed to the ministry in 1741, accepted his first parish, and was ordained a year later, in 1742.

Blair's preaching rather quickly became widely recognized for its interest and inspiration to his hearers, and in 1743 he became a preacher at Cannongate. He was later given the second position at St. Giles, which he kept until his death. In 1774, Blair was finally persuaded by Lord Kames to publish his *Sermons*, which, with the help to publication by Samuel Johnson, were wildly popular in Scotland and England, even to the point of endorsement by the King and Queen. Blair was a leading light of the Scottish Moderate clergy, a faction within the Presbyterian Church emphasizing the social and unitive nature of Christianity, and defending, as inherent to Christianity and Protestant theology, the principle of intellectual freedom.

Blair was also a central figure in the literary and intellectual circles of Edinburgh. He was close friends to many of the Scottish Enlightenment thinkers, including David Hume, Lord Kames, Thomas Reid, John Robertson, Adam Smith, and Alexander Wedderburn, among many others. With Hume, in particular, he remained intimate friends for the whole of their lives. Although a committed Conservative and leading Moderate within the church, Blair at several points took some pains to write in defence of his and Lord Kames's work against charges of heresy. Like most of the authors in this volume, he believed in and assisted the case for religious toleration. He was an active member of Edinburgh's many Societies, and was widely sought for his critique and advice on texts. He also championed James MacPherson's Ossian works, believing them to be genuine, and of great importance to forming the Scottish literary tradition. He later also supported Robert Burns, who writes about him with affection.

In 1759, Blair took over Adam Smith's public lectures on Rhetoric and Belles Lettres. A year later, the Edinburgh Town Council (which controlled both the High School and the University) voted to create for Blair the first Professor of Rhetoric at Edinburgh University. Royal decree formed for him the Regius Professorship in Rhetoric and Belles Lettres at the University of Edinburgh in 1762. It was upon his retirement in 1783 that Blair was persuaded to publish his *Lectures on Rhetoric and Belles Lettres*, in part to correct the inadequate versions based on student notes that were then being circulated. It became one of the most widely published rhetorical textbooks of all time, with more than 70 complete editions, and innumerable abridgements, adaptations, unofficial excerpts and reprints, and imitations between 1783 and the early 1800s. Its use in classrooms was intercontinental, used in translation throughout Europe and reprinted widely in America. Blair died at his home on 27 December 1800, at the age of 82.

While both his *Sermons* and his *Lectures* were extremely successful and widely read, it is hard not to argue that Blair's greatest influence was as a facilitator for the ideas of his warm and extensive social and academic networks. Blair was a leading figure in many areas of Scottish life at the time, and although his reputation as an arbiter of taste would later fall out of fashion, there is little contest that the achievements of the Scottish Enlightenment owes much to him.

Sources

Chalmers, Robert, 'Blair, Hugh', *Biographical Dictionary of Eminent Scotsmen,* Glasgow: Blackie and Son, 1875. Online ed. National Library of Scotland.

Ferriera-Buckley, Linda, and S. Michael Halloran, 'Introduction' to Hugh Blair, *Lectures on Rhetoric and Belles Lettres,* Carbondale: Southern Illinois University Press, 2005.

Howell, W.S., *Eighteenth-century British Logic and Rhetoric,* 1971.

Sher, Richard B., 'Blair, Hugh (1718–1800)', *Oxford Dictionary of National Biography,* Ed. H.C.G. Matthew and Brian Harrison, Oxford: Oxford University Press, 2004. Online ed., Ed. Lawrence Goldman, Oct. 2009.

READING XVI[1]

'Introduction'

One of the most distinguished privileges, which Providence has conferred upon mankind, is the power of communicating their thoughts to one another. Destitute of this power, Reason would be a solitary, and, in some measure, an unavailing principle. Speech is the great instrument by which man becomes beneficial to man: and it is to the intercourse and transmission of thought, by means of speech, that we are chiefly indebted for the improvement of thought itself. Small are the advances, which a single unassisted individual can make towards perfecting any of his powers. What we call human reason, is not the effort or ability of one, so much as it is the result of the reason of many, arising from lights mutually communicated, in consequence of discourse and writing.

---

[1] Blair, Hugh, *Lectures on Rhetoric and Belles Lettres,* Second edition, corrected, London: T. Cadell, W. Strahan; Edinburgh: W. Creech, 1785, Lecture I, pp. 1–18.

It is obvious, then, that writing and discourse are objects entitled to the highest attention. Whether the influence of the speaker, or the entertainment of the hearer, be consulted, whether utility or pleasure be the principal aim in view, we are prompted, by the strongest motives, to study how we may communicate our thoughts to one another with most advantage. Accordingly we find, that in almost every nation, as soon as language had extended itself beyond that scanty communication which was requisite for the supply of men's necessities, the improvement of discourse began to attract regard. In the language even of rude uncultivated tribes, we can trace some attention to the grace and force of those expressions, which they used when they sought to persuade or to affect. They were early sensible of a beauty in discourse, and endeavoured to give it certain decorations which experience had taught them it was capable of receiving, long before the study of those decorations was formed into a regular art.

But, among nations in a civilized state, no art has been cultivated with more care, than that of language, style, and composition. The attention paid to it may, indeed, be assumed as one mark of the progress of society towards its most improved period. For, according as society improves and flourishes, men acquire more influence over one another by means of reasoning and discourse; and in proportion as that influence is felt to enlarge, it must follow, as a natural consequence, that they will bestow more care upon the methods of expressing their conceptions with propriety and eloquence. Hence we find that in all the polished nations of Europe this study has been treated as highly important, and has possessed a considerable place in every plan of liberal education.

Indeed, when the arts of speech and writing are mentioned, I am sensible that prejudices against them are apt to rise in the minds of many. A sort of art is immediately thought of, that is ostentatious and deceitful; the minute and trifling study of words alone; the pomp of expression; the studied fallacies of rhetoric; ornament substituted in the room of use. We need not wonder, that, under such imputations, all study of discourse as an art, should have suffered in the opinion of men of understanding: and I am far from denying, that rhetoric and criticism have sometimes been so managed as to tend to the corruption, rather than to the improvement, of good taste and true eloquence. But sure it is equally possible to supply the principles of reason and good sense to this art, as to any other that is cultivated among men. If the following Lectures have any merit, it will consist in an endeavour to substitute the application of these principles in the place of artificial kind scholastic rhetoric; in an endeavour to explode false ornament, to direct attention more towards substance than show, to recommend good sense as the foundation of all good composition, and simplicity as essential to all true ornament.

When entering on the subject, I may be allowed on this occasion to suggest a few thoughts concerning the importance and advantages of such studies, and the rank they are entitled to possess in academic education. I am under no temptation, for this purpose, of extolling their importance at the expense of any other department of science. On the contrary, the study of Rhetoric and Belles Lettres supposes and requires a proper acquaintance with the rest of the liberal arts. It embraces them all within its circle, and recommends them to the highest regard.

The first care of all such as wish either to write with reputation, or to speak in public so as to command attention, must be, to extend their knowledge; to lay in a rich store of ideas relating to those subjects of which the occasions of life may call them to discourse or to write. Hence, among the ancients, it was a fundamental principle, and frequently inculcated, 'Quod omnibus disciplinis et artibus debet esse instructus orator'; that the orator ought to be an accomplished scholar, and conversant in every part of learning. It is indeed impossible to contrive an art, and very pernicious it were if it could be contrived, which should give the stamp of merit to any composition rich or splendid in expression, but barren or erroneous in thought. They are the wretched attempts towards an art of this kind which have so often disgraced oratory, and debased it below its true standard. The graces of composition have been employed to disguise or to supply the want of matter; and the temporary applause of the ignorant has been courted, instead of the lasting approbation of the discerning. But such imposture can never maintain its ground long. Knowledge and science must furnish the materials that form the body and substance of any valuable composition. Rhetoric serves to add the polish; and we know that none but firm and solid bodies can be polished well.

Of those who peruse the following Lectures, some, in consequence either of their profession, or of their prevailing inclination, may have the view of being employed in composition, or in public speaking. Others, without any prospect of this kind, may wish only to improve their taste with respect to writing and discourse, and to acquire principles which will enable them to judge for themselves in that part of literature called the Belles Lettres.

With respect to the former, such as may have occasion to communicate their sentiments to the Public, it is abundantly clear that some preparation of study is requisite for the end which they have in view. To speak or to write perspicuously and agreeably, with purity, with grace and strength, are attainments of the utmost consequence to all who propose, either by speech or writing, to address the Public. For without being master of those attainments, no man can do justice to his own conceptions; but how rich soever he may be in knowledge and in good sense, will be able to avail himself less of those treasures than such as possess not half his store, but who can display what they possess with more propriety. Neither are these attainments of that kind for which we are indebted to nature merely. Nature has, indeed, conferred upon some a very favourable distinction in this respect, beyond others. But in these, as in most other talents she bestows, she has left much to be wrought out by every man's own industry. So conspicuous have been the reflects of study and improvement in every part of eloquence; such remarkable examples have appeared of persons surmounting, by their diligence, the disadvantages of the most untoward nature, that among the learned it has long been a contested, and remains still an undecided point, whether nature or art confer most towards excelling in writing and discourse.

With respect to the manner in which art can most effectually furnish assistance for such a purpose, there may be diversity of opinions. I by no means pretend to say that mere rhetorical rules, how just soever, are sufficient to form an orator. Supposing natural genius to be favourable, more by a great deal will depend upon private application and study, than upon any system of instruction that is capable of being publicly communicated. But at the same time, though rules and instructions cannot do all that is requisite, they may, however, do much that is of real use. They cannot, it is true, inspire genius; but they can direct and assist it. They cannot remedy barrenness; but they may correct redundancy. They point out proper models for imitation. They bring into view the chief beauties that ought to be studied, and the principal faults that ought to be avoided; and thereby tend to enlighten taste, and to lead genius from unnatural deviations, into its proper channel. What would not avail for the production of great excellencies, may at least serve to prevent the commission of considerable errors.

All that regards the study of eloquence and composition, merits the higher attention upon this account that it is intimately connected with the improvement of our intellectual powers. For I must be allowed to say, that when we are employed, after a proper manner, in the study of composition, we are cultivating reason itself. True rhetoric and sound logic are very nearly allied. The study of arranging and expressing our thoughts with propriety, teaches to think, as well as to speak, accurately. By putting our sentiments into words, we always conceive them more distinctly. Every one who has the slightest acquaintance with composition knows, that when he expresses himself ill on any subject, when his arrangement is loose, and his sentences become feeble, the defects of his style can, almost on every occasion, be traced back to his indistinct conception of the subject: so close is the connection between thoughts and the words in which they are clothed.

The study of composition, important in itself at all times, has acquired additional importance from the taste and manners of the present age. It is an age wherein improvements, in every part of science, have been prosecuted with ardour. To all the liberal arts much attention has been paid; and to none more than to the beauty of language, and the grace and elegance of every kind of writing. The public ear is become refined. It will not easily bear what is slovenly and incorrect. Every author must aspire to some merit in expression, as well as in sentiment, if he would not incur the danger of being neglected and despised.

I will not deny that the love of minute elegance, and attention to inferior ornaments of composition, may at present have engrossed too great a degree of the public regard. It is indeed my opinion, that we lean to this extreme; often more careful of polishing style, than of storing it with thought. Yet hence arises a new reason for the study of just and proper composition. If it be requisite not to be deficient in elegance or ornament in times when they are in such high estimation, it is still more requisite to attain the power of distinguishing false ornament from true, in order to prevent our being carried away by that torrent of false and frivolous taste, which never fails, when it is prevalent, to sweep along with it the raw and the ignorant. They who have never studied eloquence in its principles, nor have been trained to attend to the genuine and manly beauties of good writing are always ready to be caught by the mere glare of language; and when they come to speak in public, or to compose, have no other standard on which to format themselves, except what chances to be fashionable and popular, however corrupted or erroneous that may be.

But as there are many who have no such objects as either composition or public speaking in view, let us next consider what advantages may be derived by them, from such studies as form the subject of these Lectures. To them, rhetoric is not so much a practical art as a speculative science; and the same instructions, which assist others in composing, will assist them in discerning, and relishing, the beauties of composition. Whatever enables genius to execute well, will enable taste to criticize justly.

When we name criticizing, prejudices may perhaps arise, of the same kind with those which I mentioned before with respect to rhetoric. As rhetoric has been sometimes thought to signify nothing more than the scholastic study of words, and phrases, and tropes, so criticism has been considered as merely the art of finding faults; as the frigid application of certain technical terms, by means of which persons are taught to cavil and censure in a learned manner. But this is the criticism of pedants only. True criticism is a liberal and humane art. It is the offspring of good sense and refined taste. It aims at acquiring a just discernment of the real merit of authors. It promotes a lively relish of their beauties, while it preserves us from that blind and implicit veneration which would confound their beauties and auks in our esteem. It teaches us, in a word, to admire and to blame with judgment, and not to follow the crowd blindly.

In an age when works of genius and literature are so frequently the subjects of discourse, when every one erects himself into a judge, and when we can hardly mingle in polite society without bearing some share in such discussions; studies of this kind, it is not to be doubted, will appear to derive part of their importance am the use to which they may be applied in furnishing materials for those fashionable topics of discourse, and thereby enabling us to support a proper rank in social life.

But I should be sorry if we could not rest the merit of such studies on somewhat of solid and intrinsical use, independent of appearance and show. The exercise of taste and of sound criticism, is in truth one of the most improving employments of the understanding. To apply the principles of good sense to composition and discourse; to examine what is beautiful, and why it is so; to employ ourselves in distinguishing accurately between the specious and the solid, between affected and natural ornament, must certainly improve us not a little in the most valuable part fall philosophy, the philosophy of human nature. For such disquisitions are very intimately connected with the knowledge of ourselves. They necessarily lead us to reflect on the operations of the imagination, and the movements of the heart; and increase our acquaintance with some of the most refined feelings which belong to our frame.

Logical and ethical disquisitions move in a higher sphere, and are conversant with objects of a more severe kind: the progress of the understanding in its search after knowledge, and the direction of the will in the proper pursuit of good. They point out to man the improvement of his nature as an intelligent being; and his duties as the subject of moral obligation. Belles Lettres and criticism chiefly consider him as a Being endowed with those powers of taste and imagination, which were intended to embellish his mind, and to supply him with rational and useful entertainment. They open a field of investigation peculiar to themselves. All that relates to beauty, harmony, grandeur, and elegance; all that can sooth the mind, gratify the fancy, or move the affections, belongs to their province. They present human nature under a different aspect from that which it assumes when viewed by other sciences. They bring to light various springs of action, which, without their aid, might have passed unobserved; and which, though of a delicate nature, frequently exert a powerful influence on several departments of human life.

Such studies have also this peculiar advantage, that they exercise our reason without fatiguing it. They lead to inquiries acute, but not painful; profound, but not dry nor abstruse. They strew flowers in the path of science; and while they keep the mind bent in some degree, and active, they relieve it at the same time from that more toilsome labour to which it must submit in the acquisition of necessary erudition, or the investigation of abstract truth.

The cultivation of taste is farther recommended by the happy effects which it naturally tends to produce on human life. The most busy man, in the most active sphere, cannot be always occupied by business. Men of serious professions cannot always be on the stretch of serious thought. Neither can the most gay and flourishing situations of fortune afford any man the power of filling all his hours with pleasure. Life must always languish in the hands of the idle. It will frequently languish even in the hands of the busy, if they have not some employment subsidiary to that which forms their main pursuit. How then shall these vacant spaces, those unemployed intervals which more or less occur in the life of every one be filled up? How can we contrive to dispose of them in any way that shall be more agreeable in itself, or more consonant to the dignity of the human mind than in the entertainments of taste, and the study of polite literature? He who is so happy as to have acquired a relish for these, has always at hand an innocent and irreproachable amusement for his leisure hours, to save him from the danger of many a pernicious passion. He is not in hazard of being a burden to himself. He is not obliged to fly to low company, or to court the riot of loose pleasures, order to cure the tediousness of existence.

Providence seems plainly to have pointed out this useful purpose to which pleasures of taste may be applied, by interposing them in a middle station between the pleasures of sense, and those of pure intellect. We were not designed to grovel always among objects so low as the former; nor are we capable of dwelling constantly in so high a region as the latter. The pleasures of taste refresh the mind after toils of the intellect, and the labours of abstract study; and they gradually raise above the attachments of sense, and prepare it for the enjoyments of virtue.

So consonant is this to experience, that, in the education of youth, no object in every age appeared more important to wise men, than to tincture them early a relish for the entertainments of taste. The transition is commonly made from these to the discharge of the higher and more important duties of life, hopes may be entertained of those whose minds have this liberal and elegant. It is favourable to many virtues. Whereas, to be entirely devoid of relish for eloquence, poetry, or any of the fine arts, is justly construed to be an unpromising symptom of youth; and raises suspicions of their being prone to low gratification destined to drudge in the more vulgar and illiberal pursuits of life.

There are indeed few good dispositions of any kind with which the improvement of taste is not more or less connected. A cultivated taste increases sensibility to all the tender and humane passions, by giving them frequent exercise; while it tends to weaken the more violent and fierce emotions.

Ingenuas didicisse fideliter artes
Emollit mores, nec sinit esse feros.[2]

The elevated sentiments and high examples which poetry, eloquence and history are often bringing under our view, naturally tend to nourish in our minds public spirit, the love of glory, contempt of external fortune, and the admiration of what is truly illustrious and great.

---

[2] Blair's Footnote: 'These polish'd arts have humanized mankind, Softend the rude, and calm'd the boist'rous mind.' [Ovid, *Epistulae Ex Ponto*, 2.9. 47–8.]

I will not go so far as to say that the improvement of taste and of virtue is the same; or that they may always be expected to coexist in an equal degree. More powerful correctives than taste can apply, are necessary for reforming the corrupt propensities which too frequently prevail among mankind. Elegant speculations are sometimes found to float on the surface of the mind, while bad passions possess the interior regions of the heart. At the same time this cannot but be admitted, that me exercise of taste is, in its native tendency, moral and purifying. From reading the most admired productions of genius, whether in poetry or prose, almost every one rises with some good impressions left on his mind; and though these may not always be durable, they are at least to be ranked among the means disposing the heart to virtue. One thing is certain, and I shall hereafter have occasion to illustrate it more fully, that, without possessing the virtuous affections to a degree, no man can attain eminence in the sublime parts of eloquence, or feel what a good man feels, if he expects greatly to move, or to interest mankind. They are the ardent sentiments of honour, virtue, magnanimity, and public spirit that only can kindle that fire of genius, and call up into the mind those high ideas, which attract the admiration of ages; and if this spirit be necessary to produce the most distinguished efforts of eloquence, it must be necessary also to our relishing them with proper taste and feeling.

On these general topics I shall dwell no longer; but proceed directly to the consideration of the subjects which are to employ the following Lectures. They divide themselves into five parts. First, some introductory dissertations on the Nature of Taste, and upon the sources of its pleasures; Secondly, the consideration language; Thirdly, of Style; Fourthly, of Eloquence properly so called; or Public Speaking in its different kinds. Lastly, a critical examination of the most distinguished Species of Composition, both in prose and verse.

READING XVII[3]

Lecture II: 'Taste'

The nature of the present undertaking leads me to begin with some enquiries concerning taste, as it is this faculty which is always appealed to in disquisitions concerning the merit of discourse and writing.

There are few subjects on which men talk more loosely and indistinctly than on taste; few, which it is more difficult to explain with precision; and none which in this course of lectures will appear more dry or abstract. What I have to say on the subject shall be in the following order. I shall first explain the nature of taste as a power or faculty in the human mind. I shall next consider how far it is an improvable faculty. I shall shew the sources of its improvement, and the characters of taste in its most perfect state. I shall then examine the various fluctuations to which it is liable, and inquire whether there be any standard to which we can bring the different tastes of men, in order to distinguish the corrupted from the true.

Taste may be defined 'The power of receiving pleasure from the beauties of nature and of art'. The first question that occurs concerning it is, whether it is to be considered as an internal sense, or as an exertion of reason? Reason is a very general term; but if we understand by it that power of the mind which in speculative matters discovers truth, and in practical matters judges of the fitness of means to an end, I apprehend the question may be easily answered. For nothing can be more clear, than that taste is not resolvable into any such operation of reason.

It is not merely through a discovery of the understanding, or a deduction of argument, that the mind receives pleasure from a beautiful prospect or a fine poem. Such objects often strike us intuitively, and make a strong impression, when we are unable to assign the reasons of our being pleased. They sometimes strike in the same manner the philosopher and

---

[3] Blair, Hugh, *Lectures on Rhetoric and Belles Lettres*, Second Edition, corrected, London: T. Cadell, W. Strahan; Edinburgh: W. Creech, 1785, Lecture II, pp. 20–43.

the peasant; the boy and the man. Hence the faculty by which we relish such beauties seems more nearly allied to a feeling of sense, than to a process of the understanding: and accordingly, from an external sense it has borrowed its name; that sense by which we receive and distinguish the pleasures of food having, in several languages, given rise to the word 'taste' in the metaphorical meaning under which, we now consider it. However, as, in all subjects which regard the operations of the mind, the inaccurate use of words is to be carefully avoided, it must not be inferred from what I have said, that Reason is entirely excluded from the exertions of taste. Though taste, beyond doubt, be ultimately founded on a certain natural and instinctive sensibility to beauty, yet reason, as I shall show hereafter, assists taste in many of its operations, and serves to enlarge its power.

Taste, in the sense in which I have explained it, is a faculty common in some degree to all men. Nothing that belongs to human nature is more general than the relish of beauty of one kind or other; of what is orderly, proportioned, grand, harmonious, new, or sprightly. In children, the rudiments of taste discover themselves very early in a thousand instances; in their fondness for regular bodies, their admiration of pictures and statues, and imitations of all kinds; and their strong attachment to whatever is new or marvellous. The most ignorant peasants are delighted with ballads and tales, and are struck with the beautiful appearances of nature in the earth and heavens. Even in the deserts of America, where human nature shews itself in its most uncultivated state, the savages have their ornaments of dress, their war and their death songs, their harangues, and their orators. We must therefore conclude the principles of taste to be deeply founded in the human mind. It is no less essential to man to have some discernment of beauty, than it is to possess the attributes of reason and of speech.

But although none be wholly devoid of this faculty, yet the degrees in which it is possessed are widely different. In some men only the feeble glimmerings of taste appear; the beauties which they relish are of the coarsest kind; and of these they have but a weak and confused impression. In others, Taste rises to an acute discernment, and a lively enjoyment of the most refined beauties. In general, we may observe that in the powers and pleasures of taste, there is a more remarkable inequality among men, than is usually found in point of common sense, reason, and judgment. The constitution of our nature in this, as in all other respects, discovers admirable wisdom. In the distribution of those talents which necessary for man's well-being, nature hath made less distinction among her children. But in the distribution of those which belong only to the ornamental part of life, she has bestowed her favours with more frugality. She has both sown the seeds more sparingly; and rendered a higher culture requisite for bringing them to perfection.

This inequality of taste among men is owing, without doubt, in part, to the different frame of their natures; to nicer organs, and finer internal powers, with which some are endowed beyond others. But, if it be owing in part to nature, it owing to education and culture still more. The illustration of this leads to my next remark on this subject, that taste is a most improvable faculty, if there be any such in human nature, a remark which gives great encouragement to such a course of study as we are now proposing to pursue. Of the truth of this assertion we may easily be convinced, by only reflecting on that immense superiority which education and improvement give to civilized, above barbarous nations, in refinement of taste; and on the superiority which they give in the same nation to those who have studied the liberal arts, above the rude and untaught vulgar. The difference is so great, that there is perhaps no one particular in which these two classes of men are so far removed from each other, as in respect of the powers and the pleasures of taste: and assuredly for this difference no other general cause can be impugned but culture and education. I shall now proceed to shew what the means, by which taste becomes so remarkably susceptible of cultivation and progress. Reflect first upon that great law of our nature, that exercise is the chief source improvement in all our faculties. This holds both in our bodily, and in our mental powers. It holds even in our external senses; although these be less the object of cultivation than any of our other faculties. We see how acute the senses some in persons whose trade or business leads to nice exertions of them. Touch, instance, becomes infinitely more exquisite in men whose employment requires them to examine the polish of bodies, than it is in others. They who deal in microscopical observations, or are accustomed to engrave on precious stones, acquire surprising accuracy of sight in discerning the minutest objects; and practice in attending to different flavours and tastes of liquors, wonderfully improves the power of distinguishing them and of tracing their composition. Placing internal taste therefore on the footing of a simple sense, it cannot be doubted that frequent exercise, and curious attention to its proper objects must greatly heighten power. Of this we have one clear proof in that part of taste, which is called an ear for music. Experience every day shews, that nothing is more improvable. Only the simplest and plainest compositions are relished at first; use and practice extend our pleasure; teach us to relish finer melody, and by degrees enable us to enter to the intricate and compounded pleasures of harmony. So an eye for the beauties painting is never all at once acquired. It is gradually formed by being conversant among pictures, and studying the works of the best masters.

Precisely in the same manner, with respect to the beauty of composition and discourse, attention to the most approved models, study of the best authors, comparisons of lower and higher degrees of the same beauties, operate towards the refinement of taste. When one is only beginning his acquaintance with works of genius, the sentiment which attends them is obscure and confused. He cannot point out the several excellencies or blemishes of a performance which he peruses; he is at a loss on what to rest his judgment; all that can be expected is, that he should tell in general whether he be pleased or not. But allow him more experience in works of this kind, and his taste becomes by degrees more exact and enlightened. He begins to perceive not only the character of the whole, but the beauties and defects of each part; and is able to describe the peculiar qualities which he praises or blames. The mist is dissipated which seemed formerly to hang over the object; and he can at length pronounce firmly, and without hesitation, concerning it. Thus in taste, considered as mere sensibility, exercise opens a great source of improvement.

But although taste be ultimately founded on sensibility, it must not be considered as instinctive sensibility alone.

Reason and good sense, as I before hinted, have so extensive an influence on all the operations and decisions of taste, that a thorough good Taste may well be considered as a power compounded of natural sensibility to beauty, and of improved understanding. In order to be satisfied of this, let us observe, that the greater part of the productions of genius are no other than imitations of nature; representations of the characters, actions, or manners of men. The pleasure we receive from such imitations or representations is founded on mere taste: but to judge whether they be properly executed, belongs to the understanding, which compares the copy with the original.

In reading for instance such a poem as the *Aenied* great part of our pleasure arises from the plan or story being well conducted, and all the parts joined together with probability and due connexion; from the characters being taken from nature, the sentiments being suited to the characters, and the style to the sentiments. The pleasure which arises from a poem so conducted is felt or enjoyed by taste as an internal sense, but the discovery of this conduct in the poem is owing to reason. The more that reason enables us to discover such propriety in the conduct, the greater will be our pleasure. We are pleased, through our natural sense of beauty. Reason shows us why, and upon what grounds, we are pleased. Wherever, in works of taste, any resemblance to nature is aimed at, wherever there is any reference of parts to a whole, or of means to an end, as there is indeed in almost every writing and discourse: there the understanding must always have a great part to act.

Here, then, is a wide field for reasons exerting its powers in relation to the objects of taste, particularly with respect to composition, and works of genius; and hence arises a second and a very considerable source of the improvement of taste, from the application of reason and good sense to such productions of genius. Spurious beauties, such as unnatural characters, forced sentiments, affected style, may please for a little; but they please only because their opposition to nature and to good sense has not been examined, or attended to. They once show how nature might have been more justly imitated or represented; how the writer might have managed his subject to greater advantage; the illusion will presently be dissipated, and these false beauties will please no more.

From these two sources then, first, the frequent exercise of taste, and next the application of good sense and reason to the objects of taste, it as a power of the mind receives its improvement. In its perfect state, it is undoubtedly the result both of nature and of art. It supposes our natural sense of beauty to be refined by frequent attention to the most beautiful objects, and at the same time to be guided and improved by the light of the understanding.

I must be allowed to add, that as a sound head, so likewise a good heart, is a very material requisite to just taste. The moral beauties are not only in themselves superior to all others, but they exert an influence, either more near or more remote, on a great variety of other objects of taste. Wherever the affections, characters, or actions of men are concerned (and these certainly afford the noblest subjects to genius), there can be neither any just or affecting description of them, nor any thorough feeling of the beauty of that description, without our possessing the unctuous affections. He whose heart is indelicate or hard, he who has no admiration of what is truly noble or praiseworthy, nor the proper sympathetic sense of what is soft and tender, must have a very imperfect relish of the highest beauties of eloquence and poetry.

The characters of taste when brought to its most improved state are all reduce to two, delicacy and correctness.

Delicacy of taste respects principally the perfection of that natural sensibility which taste is founded. It implies those finer organs or powers which enable to discover beauties that lie hid from a vulgar eye. One may have strong sensibility, and yet be deficient in delicate taste. He may be deeply impressed by such beauties as he perceives; but he perceives only what is in some degree coarse, what bold and palpable; while chaster and simpler ornaments escape his notice. In this state taste generally exists among rude and unrefined nations. But a person of delicate taste both feels strongly, and feels accurately. He sees distinctions and differences where others see none; the most latent beauty does not escape him and he is sensible of the smallest blemish. Delicacy of taste is judged of by the same marks that we use in judging of the delicacy of an external sense. As the goodness of the palate is not tried by strong flavours, but by a mixture of ingredients, where, notwithstanding the confusion, we remain sensible of each. In like manner, delicacy of internal taste appears by a quick and lively sensibility to its sense most compounded, or most latent objects.

Correctness of taste respects chiefly the improvement which that faculty receives through its connection with the understanding. A man of correct taste is he who is never imposed on by counterfeit beauties; who carries always in his mind that standard of good sense which he employs in judging of every thing. He estimates with propriety the comparative merit of the several beauties which he meets with in any work of genius; refers them to their proper classes; assigns the principles, as far as they can be traced, whence their power of pleasing flows; and is pleased himself precisely in that degree in which he ought, and no more.

It is true that these two qualities of taste—delicacy and correctness—mutually supply each other. No taste can be exquisitely delicate without being correct; nor be thoroughly correct without being delicate. But still a predominancy of one or an other quality in the mixture is often visible. The power of delicacy is chiefly seen in discerning the true merit of a work; the power of correctness, in rejecting false pretensions to merit. Delicacy leans more to feeling; Correctness more to reason and judgment. The former is more the gift of nature; the latter, more the product of culture and art. Among the ancient critics, Longinus possessed most delicacy; Aristotle, most correctness. Among the moderns, Mr. Addison is a high example of delicate taste; Dean Swift, had he written on the subject of criticism, would perhaps have afforded the example of a correct one.

Having viewed taste in its most improved and perfect state, I come next to consider its deviations from that state, the fluctuations and changes to which it is liable; and to inquire whether, in the midst of these, there be any means of distinguishing a true from a corrupted taste. This brings us to the most difficult part of our task. For it must be acknowledged, that no principle of the human mind is, in its operations, more fluctuating and capricious than taste. Its variations have been so great and frequent, as to create a suspicion with some, of its being merely arbitrary; grounded on no foundation, ascertainable by no standard, but wholly dependent on changing fancy; the consequence of which would be, that all studies or regular inquiries concerning the objects of taste were vain. In architecture, the Grecian models were long esteemed the most perfect. In succeeding ages, the Gothic architecture alone prevailed, and afterwards the Grecian taste revived in all its vigour, and engrossed the public admiration. In eloquence and poetry, the Asiatics at no time relished any thing but what was full of ornament, and splendid in a degree that we should denominate gawdy; whilst the Greeks admired only chaste and simple beauties, and despised the Asiatic ostentation. In our own country, how many writings that were greatly extolled two or three centuries ago, are now fallen into entire disrepute and oblivion? Without going back to remote instances, how very different is the taste of poetry which prevails in Great Britain now, from what prevailed there no longer ago than the reign of King Charles II, which the authors of that time too deemed an Augustan age: when nothing was in vogue but an affected brilliancy of wit; when the simple majesty of Milton was overlooked, and *Paradise Lost* almost entirely unknown; when Cowley's laboured and unnatural conceits were admired as the very quintessence of genius; Waller's gay sprightliness was mistaken for the tender spirit of Love poetry; and such writers as Suckling and Etheridge were held in esteem for dramatic composition?

The question is, what conclusion we are to form from such instances as these? Is there any thing that can be called a standard of taste, by appealing to which we may distinguish between a good and a bad taste? Or, is there in truth no such distinction; and are we to hold that, according to the proverb, there is no disputing of tastes; but that whatever pleases is right, for that reason that it does please? This is the question, and a very nice and subtle one it is, which we are now to discuss.

I begin by observing, that if there be no such thing as any standard of taste, this consequence must immediately follow, that all tastes are equally good; a position, which though it may pass unnoticed in slight matters, and when we speak of the lesser differences among the tastes of men, yet when we apply it to the extremes, presently shows its absurdity. For is there any one who will seriously maintain that the taste of a Hottentot or a Laplander is as delicate and as correct as that of a Longinus or an Addison? Or, that he can be charged with no defect or incapacity who thinks a common newswriter as excellent an historian as Tacitus? As it would be held downright extravagance to talk in this manner, we are led unavoidably to this conclusion, that there is some foundation for the preference of one man's taste to that of another; or, that there is a good and a bad, a right and a wrong in taste, as in other things.

But to prevent mistakes on this subject, it is necessary to observe next, that diversity of tastes which prevails among mankind, does not in every case ensure corruption of taste, or oblige us to seek for some standard in order to determine who are in the right. The tastes of men may differ very considerably as to their object, and yet none of them be wrong. One man relishes poetry most; another takes pleasure in nothing but history. One prefers comedy; another, tragedy. One admires the simple; another, the ornamented style. The young are used with gay and sprightly compositions. The elderly are more entertained by those of a graver cast. Some nations delight in bold pictures of manners, and some representations of passion. Others incline to more correct and regular eloquence both in description and sentiment. Though all differ, yet all pitch upon one beauty which peculiarly suits their turn of mind, and therefore no one a title to condemn the rest. It is not in matters of taste, as in questions of mere son, where there is but one conclusion that can be true, and all the rest are harmonious. Truth, which is the object of reason, is one; beauty, which is the object of taste, is manifold. Taste therefore admits of latitude and diversity of objects in sufficient consistency with goodness or justness of taste.

But then, to explain this matter thoroughly, I must observe farther, that this permissible diversity of tastes can only have place where the objects of taste are different. Where it is with respect to the same object that men disagree, when one condemns that as ugly, which another admires as highly beautiful; then it is no longer diversity, but direct opposition of taste that takes place; and therefore one must be in the right, and another in the wrong, unless that absurd paradox were owed to hold, that all Tastes are equally good and true. One man prefers Virgil to Homer. Suppose that I, on the other hand, admire Homer more than Virgil. I have as yet no reason to say that our tastes are contradictory. The other person is most struck with the elegance and tenderness which are the characteristics of Virgil; with the simplicity and fire of Homer. As long as neither of us deny that both Homer and Virgil have great beauties, our difference falls within the compass of at diversity of Tastes, which I have shewed to be natural and allowable. But if the other man shall assert that Homer has no beauties whatever; that he holds him to be a dull and spiritless writer, and that he would as soon peruse any old legend of Knight-errantry as the *Iliad*; then I exclaim, that my antagonist either void of all taste, or that his taste is corrupted in a miserable degree; and I appeal to whatever I think the standard of taste, to show him that he is in the wrong.

What that standard is, to which, in such opposition of tastes, we are obliged to have recourse, remains to be traced. A standard properly signifies, that which of such undoubted authority as to be the test of other things of the same kind. Thus a standard weight or measure, is that which is appointed by law to regulate all other measures and weights. Thus the court is said to be the standard of good breeding; and the scripture, of theological truth.

When we say that nature is the standard of taste, we lay down a principle very true and just, as far as it can be applied. There is no doubt, that in all cases where an imitation is intended of some object that exists in nature, as in representing human characters or actions, conformity to nature affords a full and distinct criterion of what is truly beautiful. Reason hath in such cases full scope for exerting its authority for approving or condemning by comparing the copy with the original. But there are innumerable cases in which this rule cannot be at all applied; and conformity to nature is an expression frequently used without any distinct or determinate meaning. We must therefore search for somewhat that can be rendered more clear and precise to be the standard of taste.

Taste, as I before explained it, is ultimately founded on an internal sense of beauty, which is natural to men, and which, in its application to particular objects, is capable of being guided and enlightened by reason. Now, were there any one person who possessed in full perfection all the powers of human nature, whose internal senses were in every instance exquisite and just, and whose reason was unerring and sure, the determinations of such a person concerning beauty, would beyond doubt, be a perfect standard for the taste of all others. Wherever their taste differed from his, it could be imputed only to some imperfection in their natural powers. But as there is no such living standard, no one person to whom all mankind will allow such submission to be due, what is there of sufficient authority to be the standard of the various and opposite tastes of men? Most certainly there is nothing but the taste, as far as it can be gathered, of human nature. That which men concur the most in admiring, must be held to be beautiful. His taste must be esteemed just and true, which coincides with the general sentiments of men. In this standard we must rest. To the sense of mankind the ultimate appeal must ever lie, in all works of taste. If any one should maintain that sugar was bitter and tobacco was sweet, no reasonings could avail to prove it. The taste of such a person would infallibly be held to be diseased, merely because it differed so widely from the taste of the species to which he belongs. In like manner, with regard to the objects of sentiment or internal taste, the common feelings of men carry the same authority, and have a title to regulate the taste of every individual.

But have we then, it will be said, no other criterion of what is beautiful, than the approbation of the majority? Must we collect the voices of others, before we form any judgment for ourselves, of what deserves applause in eloquence or poetry? By no means. There are principles of reason and sound judgment which can be applied to matters of taste, as well as to the subjects of science and philosophy. He who admires or censures any work of genius, is always ready, if his taste be in any degree improved, to assign some reasons of his decision. He appeals to principles, and points out the grounds on which he proceeds. Taste is a sort of compound power, in which the light of the understanding always mingles, more or less, with the feelings of sentiment.

But, though reason can carry us a certain length in judging concerning works of taste, it is not to be forgotten that the ultimate conclusions to which our reasonings lead, refer at last to sense and perception. We may speculate and argue concerning propriety of conduct in a tragedy, or an epic poem. Just reasonings on the subject will correct the caprice of unenlightened taste, and established principles for judging of what deserves praise. But, at the same time, these reasonings appeal always, in the last resort, to feeling. The foundation upon which they rest, is what has been found from experience to please mankind universally. Upon this ground we prefer a simple and natural, to an artificial and affected style; a regular and well-connected story, to loose and scattered narratives; a catastrophe which is tender and pathetic, to one which leaves us unmoved. It is from consulting our own imagination and heart, and from attending to the feelings of others, that any principles are formed which acquire authority in matters of taste.

When we refer to the concurring sentiments of men as the ultimate test of what is to be accounted beautiful in the arts, this is to be always understood of men placed in such situations as are favourable to the proper exertions of taste. Every one must perceive, that among rude and uncivilized nations, and during the ages of ignorance and darkness, any loose notions that are entertained concerning such subjects carry no authority. In those states of society taste has no materials on which to operate. It is either totally suppressed, or appears in its lowest and most imperfect form. We refer to the sentiments of mankind in polished and flourishing nations; when arts are cultivated and manners refined; when works of genius are subjected to free discussion, and taste is improved by science and philosophy.

Even among nations, at such a period of society, I admit, that accidental causes may occasionally warp the proper operations of taste; sometimes the state of religion, sometimes the form of government, may for a while pervert it; a licentious court may introduce a taste for false ornaments, and dissolute writings. The usage of one admired genius may procure approbation for his faults, and even render them fashionable. Sometimes envy may have power to bear down, for a little, productions of great merit; while popular humour, or party spirit, may, at other times, exalt to a high, though short-lived, reputation, what little deserved it. But though such casual circumstances give the appearance of caprice to the judgments of taste, that appearance is easily corrected. In the course of time, the genuine taste of human nature never fails to disclose itself, and to gain the ascendant over any fantastic and corrupted modes of taste which may chance to have been introduced. These may have currency for a while, and mislead superficial judges, but being subjected to examination, by degrees they pass away; while that alone remains which is founded on sound reason, and the native feelings of men.

I by no means pretend, that there is any standard of taste, to which, in every particular instance, we can resort for clear and immediate determination. Where indeed, is such a standard to be found for deciding any of those great controversies in reason and philosophy, which perpetually divide mankind? In the present case, there was plainly no occasion for any such strict and absolute provision to be made. In order to judge of what is morally good or evil, of what man ought, or ought not in duty to do, it was fit that the means of clear and precise determination should be afforded us. But to ascertain in every case with the utmost exactness what is beautiful or elegant, was not at all necessary to the happiness of man. And therefore some diversity in feeling was here allowed to take place; and room was left for discussion and debate, concerning the degree of approbation to which any work of genius is entitled.

The conclusion, which it is sufficient for us to rest upon, is, that taste is far from being an arbitrary principle, which is subject to the fancy of every individual, and which admits of no criterion for determining whether it be false or true. Its foundation is the same in all human minds. It is built upon sentiments and perceptions which belong to our nature; and which, in general, operate with the same uniformity as our other intellectual principles. When these sentiments are perverted by ignorance and prejudice, they are capable of being rectified by reason. Their sound and natural state is ultimately determined, by comparing them with the general taste of mankind. Let men declaim as much as they please, concerning the caprice and the uncertainty of taste, it is found, by experience, that there are beauties, which, if they be displayed in a proper light, have power to command lasting and general admiration. In every composition, what interests the imagination, and touches the heart, pleases all ages and all nations. There is a certain string, to which, when properly struck, the human heart is so made as to answer.

Hence the universal testimony which the most improved nations of the earth have conspired, throughout a long tract of ages, to give to some few works of genius; such as the *Iliad* of Homer, and the *Aenid* of Virgil. Hence the authority which such works have acquired, as standards income degree of poetical composition; since from them we are enabled to collect what the sense of mankind is, concerning those beauties which give them the highest pleasure, and which therefore poetry ought to exhibit. Authority or prejudice may, in one age or country, give a temporary reputation to an indifferent poet, or a bad artist; but when foreigners, or when posterity examine his works, his faults are discerned, and the genuine Taste of human nature appears. 'Opinionum commenta delet dies; naturae judicia confirmat.'[4] Time overthrows the illusions of opinion, but establishes the decisions of nature.

READING XVIII[5]

'Means of Improving in Eloquence'

I have now treated fully of the different kinds of public speaking, of the composition, and of the delivery of a discourse. Before I finish this subject, it may be of use to suggest some things concerning the properest means of improvement in the art of public speaking, and the most necessary studies for that purpose.

---

[4] Cicero, *De Natura*, II, 2.
[5] Blair, Hugh, *Lectures on Rhetoric and Belles Lettres*, Second Edition, corrected, London: T. Cadell, W. Strahan: Edinburgh: W. Creech, 1785, Lecture XXXIV, pp. 457–480.

Hugh Blair (1718–1800)

To be an eloquent speaker, in the proper sense of the word, is far from being either a common or an easy attainment. Indeed, to compose a florid harangue on some popular topic, and to deliver it so as to amuse an Audience, is a matter not very difficult. But though some praise be due to this, yet the idea, which I have endeavoured to give of eloquence, is much higher. It is a great exertion the human powers. It is the art of being persuasive and commanding; the art, not of pleasing the fancy merely, but of speaking both to the understanding and to the heart; of interesting the hearers in such a degree, as to seize and carry them along with us; and to leave them with a deep and strong impression of what they have heard. How many talents, natural and acquired, must concur for carrying this to perfection? A strong, lively, and warm imagination; quick sensibility of the heart, joined with solid judgment, good sense, and presence of mind; all improved by great and long attention to style and composition; and supported also by the exterior, yet important qualifications, of a graceful manner, a presence not ungainly, and a full and tuneable voice. How little reason to wonder, that a perfect and accomplished Orator should be one of the characters that is most rarely to be found?

Let us not despair, however: between mediocrity and perfection, there is very wide interval. There are many intermediate spaces, which may be filled up with honour; and the more rare and difficult that complete perfection is, the greater is the honour of approaching to it, though we do not fully attain it. The number of orators who stand in the highest class is, perhaps, smaller than the number of poets who are foremost in poetic fame; but the study of oratory has this advantage above that of poetry, that, in poetry, one must be an eminently good performer, or he is not supportable:

Mediocribus esse Poëtis
Non homines, non Di, non concessère columnar.[6]

---

[6]   Blair's footnote: For God and Man, and lettered post denies,
      That Poets ever are of middling size.

In eloquence this does not hold. There, one may possess a moderate station with dignity. Eloquence admits of a great many different forms; plain and simple, as well as high and pathetic. A genius that cannot reach the latter, may shine with much reputation and usefulness in the former.

Whether nature or art contribute most to form an orator is a trifling inquiry. In all attainments whatever, nature must be the prime agent. She must bestow the original talents. She must sow the seeds; but culture is requisite for bringing these seeds to perfection. Nature must always have done somewhat; but a great deal will always be left to be done by art. This is certain, that study and discipline are more necessary for the improvement of natural genius, in oratory, than they are in poetry. What I mean is that though poetry be capable of receiving assistance from critical art, yet a poet, without any aid from art, by the force of genius alone, can rise higher than a public speaker can do, who has never given attention to the rules of style, composition, and delivery. Homer formed himself; Demosthenes and Cicero were formed by the help of much labour, and of many assistances derived from the labour of others. After these preliminary observations, let us proceed to the main design of this Lecture: to treat of the means to be used for improvement in eloquence.

In the first place, what stands highest in the order of means, is personal character and disposition. In order to be a truly eloquent or persuasive speaker, nothing is more necessary than to be a virtuous man. This was a favourite position among the ancient rhetoricians: 'Non posse Oratorem esse nisi virum bonum.'[7] To find any such connection between virtue and one of the highest liberal arts, must give pleasure, and it can, I think, be clearly shown, that this is not a mere topic of declamation, but that the connection here alleged, is undoubtedly founded in truth and reason.

For, consider first, whether any thing contribute more to persuasion, than the opinion which we entertain of the probity, disinterestedness, candour, and other good moral qual-

---

[7] Quintilian, *Inst. Oratoria*, pre. 9, and xii.1.

ities of the person who endeavours to persuade? These give weight and force to every thing which he utters; nay, they add a beauty to it; they dispose us to listen with attention and pleasure; and create a secret partiality in favour of that side which he espouses. Whereas, if we entertain a suspicion of craft and disingenuity, of a corrupt, or a base mind, in the speaker, his eloquence loses all its real effect. It may entertain and amuse; but it is viewed as artifice, as trick, as the play only of speech; and, viewed in this light, whom can it persuade? We even read a book with more pleasure, when we think favourably of its author; but when we have the living speaker before our eyes, addressing us personally on some subject of importance the opinion we entertain of his character must have a much more powerful effect.

But, lest it should be said, that this relates only to the character of virtue, which one may maintain, without being at bottom a truly worthy man, I must observe farther, that, besides the weight which it adds to character, real virtue operates also in other ways, to the advantage of eloquence.

First, nothing is so favourable as virtue to the prosecution of honourable studies. It prompts a generous emulation to excel; it inures to industry; it leaves the mind vacant and free, master of itself, disencumbered of those bad passions, and disengaged from those mean pursuits, which have ever been found the greatest enemies to true proficiency Quintilian has touched this consideration very properly: '*Quod si agrorum nimia cura, et sollicitior rei familiaris diligentia, et venandi voluptas, & dati spectaculis dies, multum studiis auferunt, quid putamus facturas cupiditatem, avaritiam, invidiam? Nihil enim est tam occupatum, tam multiforme, tot ac tam variis affectibus concisum, atque laceratum, quam mala ac improba mens. Quis inter hæc, literis, aut ulli bonæ arti, locus? Non hercle magis quam frugibus, in terra sentibus ac rubis occupata.*'[8]

---

[8] Blair's footnote: 'If the management of an estate, if anxious attention to domestic economy, a passion for hunting, or whole days given up to public places and amusements, consume so much time that is due to study how much greater waste must be occasioned by licentious desires, avarice, or envy? Nothing is so much hurried and agitated, so contradictory to itself, or so violently torn and shattered by conflicting passions, as a bad heart. Amidst the distractions which it

But, besides this consideration, there is another of still higher importance, though I am not sure of its being attended to as much as it deserves; namely, that from the fountain of real and genuine virtue, are drawn those sentiments which will ever be most powerful in affecting the hearts of others. Bad as the world is, nothing has so great and universal a command over the minds of men as virtue. No kind of language is so generally understood, and so powerfully felt as the native language of worthy and virtuous feelings. He only, therefore, who possesses these full and strong, can speak properly, and in its own language, to the heart. On all great subjects and occasions, there is a dignity, there is an energy noble sentiments, which is overcoming and irresistible. They give an ardour and a flame to one's discourse, which seldom fails to kindle a like flame in those who hear; and which, more than any other cause, bestows on eloquence that power, for which it is famed, of seizing and transporting an audience. Here, art and imitation will not avail. An assumed character conveys nothing of this powerful warmth. It is only a native and unaffected glow of feeling, which can transmit the emotion to others. Hence, the most renowned orators, such as Cicero and Demosthenes, were no less distinguished for some of the high virtues, as public spirit and zeal for their country, than for eloquence. Beyond doubt, to these virtues their eloquence owed much of its effect; and those orations of theirs, in which there breathes most of the virtuous and magnanimous spirit, are those which have most attracted the admiration of ages.

Nothing, therefore, is more necessary for those who would excel in any of higher kinds of oratory, than to cultivate habits of the several virtues, and to fine and improve all their moral feelings. Whenever these become dead, or callous, they may be assured, that, on every great occasion, they will speak with less power, and less success. The sentiments and dispositions, particularly requisite for them to cultivate, are the following: The love of justice and order, and

---

produces, what room is left for the cultivation of letters, or the pursuit of any honourable art? No more, assuredly, than there is for the growth of corn in a field that is overrun with thorns and brambles.'

indignation at insolence and oppression; the love of honesty and truth, and detestation of fraud, meanness, and corruption; magnanimity of spirit, the love of liberty, of their country and the public; zeal for all great and noble designs, and reverence for all worthy and heroic characters. A cold and sceptical turn of mind is extremely adverse to eloquence; and no less so, is that cavilling disposition which takes pleasure in depreciating what is great, and ridiculing what is generally admired. Such disposition bespeaks one not very likely to excel in any thing; but least of all in Oratory. A true Orator should be a person of generous sentiments, of warm feelings, and of a mind turned towards the admiration of all those great and high objects, which mankind are naturally formed to admire. Joined with the manly virtues, he should, at the same time, possess strong and tender sensibility to all the injuries, distresses, and sorrows, of his fellow-creatures; a heart that can easily relent; and that can readily enter into the circumstances of others, and can make their case his own. A proper mixture of courage, and of modesty, must also be studied every public speaker. Modesty is essential—it is always, and justly, supposed, to be a concomitant of merit; and every appearance of it is winning and prepossessing. But modesty ought not to run into excessive timidity. Every public speaker should be able to rest somewhat on himself; and to assume that air, not of self-complacency, but of firmness, which bespeaks a consciousness of his being thoroughly persuaded of the truth, or justice, of what he delivers; a circumstance of no small consequence for making impression on those who hear.

Next to moral qualifications, what, in the second place, is most necessary to an orator, is a fund of knowledge. Much is this inculcated by Cicero and Quintilian: '*Quod omnibus disciplinis et artibus debet esse instructus Orator.*' By which they mean, that he ought to have what we call, a Liberal Education; and to be formed by a regular study of philosophy, and the polite arts. We must never forget that,

Scribendi recte, sapere est & principium & fons.[9]

Good sense and knowledge, are the foundation of all good speaking. There is no art that can teach one to be eloquent, in any sphere, without a sufficient acquaintance with what belongs to that sphere; or if there were an art that made such pretensions, it would be mere quackery, like the pretensions of the Sophists of old, to teach their disciples to speak for and against every/subject; and would be deservedly exploded by all wise men. Attention to style, to composition, and all the arts of speech, can only assist an orator in setting off, to advantage, the stock of materials which he possesses; but the stock, the materials themselves, must be brought from other quarters than from rhetoric. He who is to plead at the Bar, must make himself thoroughly master of the knowledge of the law and of all the learning and experience that can be useful in his profession, for supporting a cause, or convincing a judge. He who is to speak from the pulpit must apply himself closely to the study of divinity, of practical religion, of morals, of human nature; that he may be rich in all the topics, both of instruction and of persuasion. He who would fit himself for being a member of the Supreme Council of the nation, or of any public assembly, must be thoroughly acquainted with the business that belongs to such assembly; he must study the forms of court, the course of procedure; and must attend minutely to all the facts that may be the subject of question or deliberation.

Besides the knowledge that properly belongs to his profession, a public speaker, if ever he expects to be eminent, must make himself acquainted, as far as his necessary occupations allow, with the general circle of polite literature. The study of poetry may be useful to him, on many occasions, for embellishing his style, for suggesting lively images, or agreeable allusions. The study of history may be still more useful to him; as the knowledge of facts, of eminent characters, and of the course of human affairs, finds place on

---

[9] Horace, 'For all good writing, Knowledge is the fountain and source.'

many occasions.[10] There are few great occasions of public speaking, in which one may not derive assistance from cultivated taste, and extensive knowledge. They will often yield him materials for proper ornament; sometimes, for argument and real use. A deficiency of knowledge, even in subjects that belong not directly to his own profession, will expose him to many disadvantages, and give better qualified rivals a great superiority over him.

Allow me to recommend, in the third place, not only the attainment of useful knowledge, but a habit of application and industry. Without this, it is impossible to excel in any thing. We must not imagine, that it is by a sort of mushroom growth, that one can rise to be a distinguished pleader, or preacher, or speaker in any assembly. It is not by starts of application, or by a few years preparation of study afterwards discontinued, that eminence can be attained. No; it can be attained only by means of regular industry grown up into a habit, and ready to be exerted on every occasion that calls for industry. This is the fixed law of our nature; and he must have a very high opinion of his own genius indeed that can believe himself an exception to it. A very wise law of our nature it is; for industry is, in truth, the great 'condimentum', the seasoning of every pleasure, without which life is doomed to languish. Nothing is so great an enemy both to honourable attainments, and to the real, to the brisk, and spirited enjoyment of life, as that relaxed state of mind which arises from indolence and dissipation. One that is destined to excel in any art, especially in the arts of speaking and writing, will be known by this more than by any other mark

---

[10] Blair's footnote: '*Imprimis vero, abundare debet Orator exemplorum copia, cum veterum, turn etiam novorum; adeo ut non modo quae conscripta sunt historiis, aut Sermonibus velut per manus tradita, quæque quotidie aguntur, debeat nösse; verùm ne ea quidem quae; a clarioribus poëtis sunt ficta negligere*' [Above all, the orator ought to have an abundant supply of examples both old and new, so much so that he ought not only know those which have been recorded in histories or in speeches as for instance those passed down hand to hand and those which are spoken daily, but also ought not neglect even those things which have been invented by the more notable poets], Quinct., L. xii, Cap. 4.

whatever, an enthusiasm for that art; an enthusiasm, which, firing his mind with the object he has in view, will dispose him to relish every labour which the means require. It was this that characterized the great men of antiquity; it is this, which must distinguish the moderns who would tread in their steps. This honourable enthusiasm, it is highly necessary for such as are studying oratory to cultivate. If youth wants it, manhood will flag miserably.

In the fourth place, attention to the best models will contribute greatly towards improvement. Every one who speaks, or writes, should, indeed, endeavour to have somewhat that is his own, that is peculiar to himself, and that characterizes his composition and style. Slavish imitation depresses genius, or rather betrays the want of it. But withal, there is no genius so original but may be profited and assisted by the aid of proper examples, in style, composition, and delivery. They always open some new ideas; they serve to enlarge and correct our own. They quicken the current of thought, and excite emulation.

Much, indeed, will depend upon the right choice of models which we purpose to imitate; and supposing them rightly chosen, a farther care is requisite, of not being seduced by a blind universal admiration. For, *'decipit exemplar, vitiis imitabile'*. Even in the most finished models we can select, it must not be forgotten, that there are always some things improper for imitation. We should study to acquire a just conception of the peculiar characteristic beauties of any writer, public speaker, and imitate these only. One ought never to attach himself too closely to any single model; for he who does so is almost sure of being seduced into a faulty and affected imitation. His business should be to draw from several the proper ideas of perfection. Living examples of public speaking, in any kind, it will not be expected that I should here point out. As to the writers ancient and modern, from whom benefit may be derived in forming composition and style, I have spoken so much of them in former Lectures, that it is needless to repeat what have said of their virtues and defects. I own, it is to be regretted, that the English language, in which there is much good writing, furnishes us, however, with but very few recorded examples of eloquent public speaking. Among the

French there are more. Saurin, Bourdaloue, Flechier, Massillon, particularly the last, are eminent for the eloquence of the Pulpit. But the most nervous and sublime of all their orators is Bossuet, the famous Bishop of Meaux; in whose *Oraisons Funebres*, there is a very high spirit of oratory.[11] Some of Fontenelle's 'Harangues to the French Academy', are elegant and agreeable. And at the bar, the printed pleadings of Cochin and D'Aguesseau, are highly extolled by the late French critics.

There is one observation which it is of importance to make, concerning imitation of the Style of any favourite author, when we would carry his style into public speaking. We must attend to a very material distinction between written and spoken language. These are, in truth, two different manners of communicating ideas. A book that is to be read, requires one sort of style; a man that is to speak, must use another. In books, we look for correctness, precision, all redundancies pruned, all repetitions avoided, language completely polished. Speaking admits a more easy copious style, and less fettered by rule; repetitions may often be necessary, parentheses may sometimes be graceful; the same thought must often be placed in different views; as the hearers can catch it only from the mouth of the Speaker, and have not the advantage, as in reading a book, of turning back again, and of dwelling on what they do not fully comprehend. Hence the style of many good authors would appear stiff, affected, and even obscure, if, by too close an imitation, we should transfer it to a popular oration. How awkward, for example, would Lord Shaftsbury's sentences sound in the mouth of a public speaker? Some kinds of public discourse, it is true, such as that of the pulpit, where more exact preparation, and more studied style are admitted, would bear such a manner

---

[11] Blair's footnote: The criticism which M. Crevier, Author of *Rhetorique Françoise*, passes upon these writers whom I have above named, is: '*Bossuet est grande, mais inégal; Flechier est plus égal, mais moins elevé, & souvent trop fleuri: Bourdaloue est solide & judicieux, mais il neglige les graces legères: Massillon est plus riche en images, mais moins fort en raisonnement. Je souhaite donc, que l'orateur ne se contente dans l'imitation d'un seul de ces modeles, mais qu'il tache de reunir en iui toutes leurs differentes vertus.*' Vol. II, chap. derniere.

better than others, which are expected to approach more to extemporaneous speaking. But still there is, in general, so much difference between speaking, and composition designed only to be read, as should guard us against a close and injudicious imitation.

Some authors there are, whose manner of writing approaches nearer to the style of Speaking than others; and who, therefore, can be imitated with more safety. In this class, among the English authors, are Dean Swift, and Lord Bolingbroke. The Dean, throughout all his writings, in the midst of much correctness, maintains the easy natural manner of an unaffected Speaker; and this is one of his chief excellencies. Lord Bolingbroke's style is more splendid, and more declamatory than Dean Swift's; but still it is the Style of one who speaks, or rather who harangues. Indeed, all his political writings (for it is to them only, and not to Philosophical ones, that this observation can be applied) carry much more appearance of one declaiming with warmth in a great assembly, than of one writing in a closet, in order to be read by others. They have all the copiousness, fervour, the inculcating method that is allowable, and graceful in an orator; perhaps too much of it for a writer: and it is to be regretted, as I have formerly; served, that the matter contained in them should have been so trivial or so for, from the manner and style, considerable advantage might be reaped.

In the fifth place, besides attention to the best models, frequent exercise in composing and speaking will be admitted to be a necessary mean of improvement. That sort of composition is, doubtless, most useful, which relates to profession, or kind of public speaking, to which persons addict themselves. This they should keep ever in their eye, and be gradually inuring themselves to it. But let me also advise them, not to allow themselves in negligent composition of a kind. He who has it for his aim to write, or to speak correctly, should, in the most trivial kind of composition, in writing a letter, nay, even in common discourse, study to acquit himself with propriety. I do not at all mean, that he is never write or to speak a word, but in elaborate and artificial language. This would form him to a stiffness and affectation, worse, by ten thousand degrees, than the greatest negligence. But it is to be observed, that there is, in every thing, a manner which

Hugh Blair (1718-1800)

is becoming, and has propriety; and opposite to it, there is a clumsy and faulty performance of the same thing. The becoming manner is very often the most light and seemingly careless manner; but it requires taste and attention to seize the just idea of it. That idea, when acquired, we should keep in our eye, and form upon it whatever we write or say.

Exercises of speaking have always been recommended to students, in order that they may prepare themselves for speaking in public, and on real business. The meetings, or Societies, into which they sometimes form themselves for this purpose, are laudable institutions; and, under proper conduct, may serve many valuable purposes. They are favourable to knowledge and study, by giving occasion to enquiries concerning those subjects which are made the ground of discussion they produce emulation; and gradually inure those who are concerned in them, to somewhat that resembles a public assembly. They accustom them to know their own powers, and to acquire a command of themselves in speaking; and what is, perhaps, the greatest advantage of all, they give them a facility and fluency of expression, and assist them in procuring that '*copia verborum*', which can be acquired by no other means but frequent exercise in speaking.

But the meetings which I have now in my eye, are to be understood of the academical associations, where a moderate number of young gentlemen, who are carrying on their studies, and are connected by some affinity in the future pursuits which they have in view, assemble privately, in order to improve one another, and to prepare themselves for those public exhibitions which may afterwards fall their lot. As for those public and promiscuous Societies, in which multitudes are brought together, who are often of low stations and occupations, who are joined by no common bond of union, except an absurd rage for public speaking, and by no other object in view, but to make a show of their supposed talents, they are institutions not merely of an useless, but of an hurtful nature. They are in great are of proving seminaries of licentiousness, petulance, faction, and folly. They mislead those who, in their own callings, might be useful members of society, into fantastic plans of making a figure on subjects which divert their attention from their proper business, and are widely remote from their sphere in life.

Even the allowable meetings into which students of oratory form themselves, stand in need of direction in order to render them useful. If their subjects of discourse be improperly chosen; if they maintain extravagant or indecent topics; if indulge themselves in loose and flimsy declamation, which has no foundation in good sense; or accustom themselves to speak pertly on all subjects without due preparation, they may improve one another in petulance, but in no other and will infallibly form themselves to a very faulty and vicious taste in speaking. I would, therefore, advise all who are members of such societies, in the first place, to attend to the choice of their subjects; that they be useful and manly, either formed on the course of their studies, or on something that has relation to morals and taste, to action and life. In the second place, I would advise them to be temperate in the practice of speaking; not to speak too often, nor on subjects where they are ignorant or unripe; but only when they have proper materials for a discourse, and have digested and thought of the subject before-hand. In the third place, when they do speak, they should study always to keep good sense and persuasion in view, rather than an ostentation of eloquence; and for this end, I would, in the fourth place, repeat the advice which I gave in a former Lecture, that they should always choose that side of the question to which, in their own judgment, they are most inclined, as the right and the true side, and defend it by such arguments as seem to them most solid. By these means, they will take the method of forming themselves gradually to a manly, correct, and persuasive manner of speaking.

It now only remains to inquire, of what use may the study of critical and rhetorical Writers be for improving one in the practice of eloquence? These are certainly not to be neglected; and yet, I dare not say that much is to be expected from them. For professed writers on public speaking, we must look chiefly among the ancients. In modern times, for reasons which were before given, popular eloquence, as an art, has never been very much the object of study; it has not the same powerful effects among us that it had in more democratical states; and therefore has not been cultivated with the same care. Among the moderns, though there has been a great deal of good criticism on the different kinds of writing, yet much has not been attempted on the subject of eloquence or public discourse; and what has been given us of that kind, has been drawn mostly from the ancients. Such writer as Joannes Gerardus Vossius, who has gathered into one heap of ponderous lumber, all the trifling, as well as the useful things, that are to be found in Greek and Roman Writers, is enough to disgust one with the study of eloquence. Among the French, there has been more attempted, on this subject, than among the English. The Bishop of Cambray's *Writings on Eloquence* I before mentioned with honour. Rollin, Batteux, Crevier, Gibert, and several other French Critics have also written on oratory; but though some of them may be useful, none of them are so considerable as to deserve particular recommendation.

It is to the original ancient writers that we must chiefly have recourse; and it is a reproach to any one, whose profession calls him to speak in public, to be unacquainted with them. In all the ancient rhetorical writers, there is, indeed, this defect, that they are too systematical, as I formerly showed; they aim at doing too much; at reducing rhetoric to a complete and perfect art, which even supply invention with materials on every subject; insomuch, that one would imagine they expected to form an orator by rule, in as mechanical a manner as one would form a carpenter. Whereas, all that can, in truth, be done, is to give openings for assisting and enlightening taste, and for pointing out to genius the course it ought to hold.

Aristotle laid the foundation for all that was afterwards written on the subject. That amazing and comprehensive genius, which does honour to human nature, and which gave light into so many different sciences, has investigated the principles of rhetoric with great penetration. Aristotle appears to have been the first who took rhetoric out of the hands of the Sophists, and introduced reasoning and good sense into the art. Some of the profoundest things which have been written on the passions and manners of men, are to be found in his *Treatise on Rhetoric*; though in this, as in all his writings, his great brevity often renders him obscure. Succeeding Greek rhetoricians, most of whom are now lost, improved on the foundation which Aristotle had laid. Two of them still remain, Demetrius Phalereus, and Dionysius of Halicarnassus; both write on the 'Construction of Sentences', and deserve to be perused; especially Dionysius, who is a very accurate and judicious critic.

I need scarcely recommend the rhetorical writings of Cicero. Whatever, on the subject of eloquence, comes from so great an orator, must be worthy of attention. His most considerable work on this subject is that *De Oratore,* in three books. None of Cicero's writings are more highly finished than this treatise. The dialogue is polite; the characters are well supported, and the conduct of the whole is beautiful and agreeable. It is, indeed, full of digressions, and his rules and observations may be thought sometimes too vague and general. Useful things, however, maybe learned from it; and it is no small benefit to be made acquainted with Cicero's own idea of eloquence. The 'Orator ad M. Brutum', is also a considerable treatise; and, in general, throughout all Cicero's rhetorical works there run those high and sublime ideas of eloquence, which are fitted both for forming a just taste, and for creating that enthusiasm for the art, which is of the greatest consequence for excelling in it.

But, of all the ancient writers on the subject of oratory, the most instructive, and most useful, is Quintilian. I know few books which abound more with good sense, and discover a greater degree of just and accurate taste, than Quintilian's *Institutions.* Almost all the principles of good criticism are to be found in them. He has digested into excellent order all the ancient ideas concerning Rhetoric, and is, at the same time, himself an eloquent Writer. Though some parts of his work contain too much of the technical and artificial system then in vogue, and for that reason may be thought dry and tedious, yet I would not advise the omitting to read any part of his *Institutions.* To Pleaders at the Bar, even these technical parts may prove of some use. Seldom has any person, of more sound and distinct judgment than Quintilian, applied himself to the study of the Art of Oratory.

Eight
Alexander Bain (1818–1903)

Alexander Bain was born on 11 June 1818, in Aberdeen. His father was a weaver, and both his parents were Calvinists. They raised their eight children in relative poverty. Bain dropped out of school at the age of eleven, but through self-directed studies and evening courses at the local mechanics institute, managed to enter Marischal College in 1836, at age 18. He graduated in 1840 with top honours in his undergraduate class, and stayed on at Marischal as a teacher of natural and moral philosophy until 1845. He was denied two chairs at this time due to objections to his lasting religious scepticism. Bain then spent a year teaching mathematics and natural philosophy at Anderson's University in Glasgow before moving to London to serve as a secretary at the Board of Health.

While in London, he associated closely with 'radical intellectual' circles including Herbert Spencer, George Eliot, John Grote, and J.S. Mill, the latter with whom he later collaborated in editing his father James Mill's *Analysis of the Phenomena of the Human Mind* (1873) and co-wrote his biography. After his retirement many years later, Bain also wrote his own critical reflections on J.S. Mill's work, *John Stuart Mill: A Criticism, and with Personal Recollections* (1882). During this period, Bain wrote on a wide variety of subjects and also travelled to Paris in 1854, meeting with intellectual circles there. He had previously secured a position teaching at Bedford College in London (a women's college), where he started his work on *The Senses and the Intellect* (1855) and *The*

Emotions and the Will (1859). Bain next moved to the University of London, where he worked as an examiner in moral science for the Indian Civil Service. He retained this position in spite of an appointment to the Chair of Logic at the newly-formed University of Aberdeen, a post he won over the objection of Colin Campbell and the Duke of Argyll, who preferred James McCosh. Bain taught in Aberdeen until his retirement in 1880, after which he remained active in civil and academic affairs until his death at his home in 1903.

Alexander Bain's legacy is complex. His body of published work is expansive, and among his great successes, including the works mentioned here as well as the founding of the influential journal *Mind*, are some remarkable failures, especially his promotion of the now-discredited science of phrenology. He is considered a founding father of psychology, as he significantly recast the mental and epistemological philosophy of Scottish Common Sensism by fusing it with the new science of the brain. Bain located mental processes within the physiological processes of the body, thus forming a new scientific method for understanding the faculties of knowing and learning. He was inclined to Mill's associationism and the new sciences of natural history, although he maintained an emphasis on the active individual will in forming habits and beliefs. Bain was an important influence on C.S. Peirce and Henry James, and his work was seminal to the next century's understanding of cognitive development in children. He himself was passionately concerned with the relationship between the psychological sciences and education, and his popular *Composition and Rhetoric* (1867, revised and expanded thereafter) demonstrates his mental and psychological theories in pedagogical action. In examining Bain's articulation of rhetoric and language use, it is essential to note the divergence of his rhetorical theory from his Common Sense predecessors. Because of Bain's firm grounding in physiological and cognitive science, what in the hands of Reid, Campbell, Gerard, and Blair was a highly philosophical approach to learning becomes in fact much more pedagogically prescriptive. For example, the proper sentence, paragraph, and essay become factual expressions of the way the mind physically operates, and thus rhetorical invention loses much of its characteristic 'probability'. This does not serve to condemn Bain's rhetorical theory as itself wholly prescriptive, but rather to point to his work as a pedagogical turning point in Scottish rhetoric.

Sources

Bain, Alexander, *Autobiography,* Elibron Classics Reprint of New York: Longman, Green, & Co. (1904), 2000.

Horner, Winifred, *Nineteenth Century Scottish Rhetoric: The American Connection,* Carbondale: Sourthern Illinois University Press, 1993.

Knight, R., 'A Bain Centenary', *Aberdeen University Review,* Vol. 36 (1955-6), pp. 160-3.

Richards, Graham, 'Alexander Bain (1818-1903)', in *Oxford Dictionary of National Biography.* Online ed., Ed. Lawrence Goldman, Oxford: Oxford University Press, 2004.

READING XIX[1]

Rhetoric discusses the means whereby language, spoken or written, may be rendered effective.

In speaking there are three principle ends — to inform, to persuade, to please. They correspond to the three departments of the human mind, the understanding, the will, and the feelings. The means being to some extent different for each, they are considered under separate heads.

But as there are various matters pertaining to all modes of address, it is convenient to divide the entire subject into the two following parts. The first part, which relates to style generally, embraces the following topics: I. *The Figures of Speech,* and the consideration of the *Number* and the *Order of Words.* II. The explanation of the various *Attributes* or *Qualities of Style.* III. The *Sentence* and the *Paragraph.*

The second part treats of the different kinds of composition. Those that have for their object to inform the understanding, fall under three heads — *Description, Narration,* and *Exposition.* The means of influencing the will are given under one head, *Persuasion.* The employing of language to excite

---

[1] From Bain, Alexander, *English Composition and Rhetoric,* Fourth Edition, London: Longmans and Green, 1877.

pleasurable feelings coincides with the most characteristic function of *Poetry*.

The will can be moved only through the understanding or through the feelings. Hence, there are at bottom but two rhetorical ends.

Style in General

The Figures of Speech

A figure of speech is a deviation from the plain and ordinary mode of speaking with a view to greater effect. When, instead of saying 'that is very strange' we exclaim 'how strange!' we use a figure. 'Now is the winter of our discontent' is figurative; the word 'winter' is diverted from signifying a season of the year to express a condition of the human feelings.

The ancient rhetoricians distinguished between figures and tropes. A figure, says Quintilian, is a *form* of speech differing from the common and ordinary mode of expression; as in the first example given above. A trope is the conversion of a *word* from its proper signification to another, in order to give force, as in the second example. The distinction is more in appearance than in substance, and has no practical value.

[…]

A classification of the important figures may be based on the operations of intellect, or understanding that they have reference to. Now, our intellectual powers are reducible to three simple modes of working.

The first is spoken under the names, *discrimination*, or feeling of difference, contrast, or relativity. It means that the mind is affected by change, as in passing from rest to motion, from cold to heat, from light to dark; and that, the greater and the more sudden the change, the stronger is the effect. The figure, denominated antithesis or contrast, derives its force from this fact.

The second power is called *similarity*, or the feeling of agreement. This signifies that when like objects come under our notice, we are impressed by circumstance, as when we see the resemblance of a child to its parent. The figures named simile, metaphor, allegory, are modes of increasing the force of style in this way.

The third power of the intellect is retentiveness, or acquisition. The ability to retain successive impressions without confusion, and to bring them up afterwards, distinguishes the mind; it is a power familiarly known by the name memory. Now, the chief way the retentiveness or memory works is this: impressions occurring together, become associated together, as sunrise with daylight; and when we are made to think of one, we are reminded of the accompaniments. We cannot think of the sun's rising, without remembering daylight, and the other circumstances that go along with it. Hence the mental association of things contiguously placed, is a prominent fact of the mind; and one of its many consequences is that we often name a thing by some one its adjuncts; as 'the throne' for the sovereign, 'gold' for wealth. Such is the nature of the metonymy.

Of the three powers of the intellect now named, discrimination or contrast, similarity, retentiveness or contiguity, the second, similarity, is the most fruitful in figures, and may be taken first in order.

The intellectual power similarity, or feeling of agreement, is the chief inventive power of mind. By it, similitudes are brought up to the view. When we look out upon a scene of nature, we are reminded of other resembling scenes that we have formerly known.

This power of like to recall like (there also being diversity) varies in different individuals. The fact is shown in great abundance of comparisons that occur to some men, as, for example, the great poets. Homer, speaking of the descent of Apollo from Olympus, says, 'He came like night.' The eloquence of Ulysses is described by the help of a similitude:

> Soft as the fleeces of descending snows
> The copious accents fall with easy art;
> Melting they fall, and sink into the heart! (*Iliad,* 95–97)

The tracing of resemblances among the objects and events of the world is a constant avocation of the human mind. It occurs largely in science.

Some sciences are expressly styled comparative: as comparative anatomy, comparative grammar. The purpose of the first is to find out the points of community or likeness among animals; the second shows the similarities occurring in the midst of diversities in languages.

The generalization, or general notions and principles constituting science, require the identification and resembling things. We identify a great number of objects on the property of roundness, all else being different; and the result is the general notion of a circle in Euclid.

Every kind of reasoning implies similarity, or the identity of two or more things. When we infer that the men now alive will die, it is because of their likeness in constitution to those that went before them. In one mode of reasoning, called reasoning by analogy, the principle is expressly indicated in the name. A comparison is often intended to serve for an argument or reason, as well as for an illustration. The following is an example.

> 'It is remarked by anatomists, that the nutritive quality is not the only requisite for food; that a certain degree of distention of the stomach is required, to enable it to act with its full powers; and that it is for reason hay or straw must be given to horses, as well corn, in order to supply the necessary bulk. Something analogous to this takes place with respect to the generality of minds; which are incapable of thoroughly digesting and assimilating what is presented to them, however clearly, in a small compass.' (Whately)[2]

In all departments of composition addressed to the understanding—in description, narration, and exposition, similitudes are made use of to render the subjects more intelligible.

If, from some cause or other, a subject is but dimly conceived by us, one mode of assisting the mind is to bring forward something of the same kind that we already understand. We then, to clear up the unfamiliar subject, transfer to it our knowledge of the familiar. Thus, the action of the heart, which is concealed from our view, may be made intelligible by comparison with a force-pump for supplying water to a town. An event in ancient history can be illustrated by something that happened in more recent times. A man's character is brought home to us when likened to some

---

[2] Whately, Richard, *Elements of Rhetoric*, Oxford: W. Baxter, 1830, p. 225.

one that we already know. We often make subjects mutually illustrative through their community of nature; thus painting and poetry, as fine arts, elucidate each other.

A resemblance is not a figure of speech, unless the things compared be different in different in kind.

[...]

In compositions addresses to the Feelings, in oratory and poetry, resemblances are sought out to give greater intensity or impressiveness to meaning.

[...]

Figures of Contrast

It is a first principle of the human mind that we are affected only by change of impression, as by passing from hot to cold, from hunger or repletion, from sound to silence. This applies to both feeling and knowledge.

Every outburst of feeling implies that we have changed from one condition to another. In some emotions, as wonder, the prominent fact is a transition from a previous state; the shock of change is the cause of the feeling. Other emotions of the same nature are Liberty, which presupposes restraint, and the sentiment of power, which is felt only by comparison with some other states of impotence or weakness.

In knowledge, likewise, there is a shock of transition. Light is known by passing out of the dark. So high, by comparison with low, hard with soft, straight with crooked, parent with child. In short, knowledge is never single; there must be at least two things. Sometimes there are more than two. Thus, 'red' is in correlation to all other colours. Our knowledge of man takes in all that we have ever contrasted with man, God, angel, etc. The essential plurality of knowledge is not fully represented in ordinary language, which usually provides only one name for one subject of discourse, as heat, man, and wisdom. We are supposed to be capable of recalling the full contrast involved in each case—heat as against cold, man-brute, etc. Still, it is not infrequently happens that our understanding of the thing is aided by the express mention of the contrasting things; this mention is therefore a device of rhetoric; and to it are applied the designations, antithesis and contrast.

So in the production of feeling: a speaker may excite the idea of liberty more strongly by conjoining, with the language usually applied to it, an explicit description of the opposite condition of restraint. The reference to the opposite contrasting state is almost unavoidable in description, but by the figure of antithesis this reference amounts to a fully-drawn picture.

The Qualities of Style

Under the great variety of descriptive words employed to signify the merits and demerits of style, we may discern a few leading qualities.

Under what has now been said regarding the number and order of words, explanations have been furnished of many characteristics of style. A composition abounding in any one of the figures would be described by that figure, as metaphorical, antithetical, epigrammatic, hyperbolic, climactic, ironic, sarcastic, or elliptical. A profusion of figurative language generally would receive the designations — figurative, flowery, ornate, imaginative, illustrative, to which are opposed plain, unfigurative, dry, bald. The reference to a number of words determines, on the one hand, the diffuse or verbose, and on the other, the terse, or concise. So a reference to the order of words would give the natural or flowing, as opposed to the inverted or involved style.

With regard to thought, or meaning, there are two chief qualities: *simplicity* and *clearness*.

As respects feeling, there is an important distinction or contrast between what is designated by the terms — *strength, energy, sublime* — and the qualities denominated *feeling, pathos,* and *beauty* (in a narrow sense); this contrast answers to the opposition of the opposite sides of our nature. To these two classes of effects, we must add the peculiar quality signified by the *ludicrous, humour,* and *wit*.

It is necessary, further, to consider the *melody* of language, and also the *expressiveness*, that is, the suiting of the sound to the sense. Finally, a few observations are needed on the meanings of *taste*.

[...]

The Meaning of Taste

The word taste, employed with reference to fine art, means, in the first instance, the susceptibility to pleasure from works of art. A person devoid of this enjoyment is said to have no taste.

There is a farther employment of the word, to denote the kind of artistic excellence that gives the greatest amount of pleasure to cultivated minds. Such minds are said to have taste, others want it. The words 'elegance', 'polish', 'refinement', designate nearly the same thing. The distinction is sometimes expressed by the epithet 'good taste', implying that taste may be bad, or enjoyment misplaced, in the judgment of those that claim to arbitrate between the two.

It being the end of rhetoric, on the whole, to consider the various points of excellence in composition, the attention to these must be synonymous with good taste. In regard to taste, there is a permanent element, and variable element.

I. The *permanent* element comprises all the rules of composition, grounded on the admitted laws of our sensibility, and generally followed by the best speakers and writers. To avoid discords, to use bold figures sparingly, to set bounds to exaggeration, to admit painful effects only so far as they can be redeemed, are the rule of taste as being rules of rhetoric.

Refinement in taste consists partly in enhancing the pleasures of works of art, by the removal of what pains, and the addition of what pleases the proper artistic sensibility; and partly it avoids the tendencies of art compositions to infringe on truth, usefulness, humane sentiment, and morality.

II. The *variable* element includes the points where men do not feel alike. Ages, countries, and individuals differ in their sense of what is excellent in composition.

Thus regards age and country—the taste of the Greeks, reverentially accepted in many things after ages, allowed to orators and to poets a license of personal vituperation that would now be condemned. Again, nothing has varied so much in different times as the mode of representing the passion of love; allusions forbidden by the taste of our day were permitted in former times.

As an example of the change of taste, compare the ancient rules of tragedy (adhered to in the French stage), which forbid the introduction of comic scenes, with the English practice in that respect. 'It was Dryden's opinion, at least for sometime, and he maintains it in the dedication to his play (The Spanish Friar), that the drama required an alternation of comic and tragic scenes; and that it is necessary to mitigate by alleviations of merriment the pressure of ponderous events, and the fatigue of toilsome passions. "Whoever," says he "cannot perform both parts, is but half a writer for the stage."' (Johnson's *Life of Dryden*.)[3]

Taste is also a matter of personal peculiarity; varying with emotional constitution, the intellectual tendencies, and the education of the individual. A person of strong tender feelings is not easily offended by the iteration of pathetic images; the sense of the ludicrous and of humour is in many cases entirely wanting; and the strength of humane and moral sentiment may be such as to recoil from inflicting ludicrous degradation. A mind bent on the pursuit of truth views with distaste the exaggerations of the poetic art. Each person is by education more attached to one school, or class or writers, than another.

---

[3] Johnson, Samuel, *The Works of English Poets, Vol. VIII*, London: 1810, p. 435.

Index of Names

Addison, Joseph, 51, 64, 157, 159
Aristophanes, 74
Aristotle, 3, 60, 65, 89, 94, 97–8, 122, 137, 157, 177–8

Bacon, Francis, 2,4, 15, 114, 119
Batteux, Charles, 177
Beattie, James, 88, 111
Beattie, John, 15
Berekely, George, 2
Berlin, James, 17
Bolingbroke, Henry St. John, Viscount, 59, 68, 174
Bossuet, Jacques-Benigne, 173
Bourdaloue, Louis, 173
Broadie, Alexander, 4
Brown, Tom, 70
Buccleuch, Duke of, 53
Burns, Robert, 17, 140

Cato, 76, 87
Campbell, Colin, 111, 180
Campbell, Margaret Walker, 111
Carmichael, Gershom, 10, 22
Charles II, King of England, 158
Cicero, Marcus Tullius, 6, 9, 61, 65, 78–87, 102, 125, 130, 132–4, 166–8, 178
Cochin, Pierre-Suzanne-Augustin, 173
Cowley, Abraham, 158
Craig, James, 43
Crevier, Jean-Baptiste-Louis, 173, 177
Cynical School, 40

D'Aguesseau, Henri-Francois, 173
Demetrius Phalerius, 178
Demosthenes, 62, 78–87, 166, 168
Dionysius of Helicarnassus, 178

Eliot, George, 179
Euclid, 127, 184
Ferriera-Buckley, Linda, 2
Flechier, Esprit, 173
Fordyce, David, 88
Fontenelle, Bernard le Bovier, 173

Goldie, John, 111
Gregory, John, 111
Grote, John, 179
Grotius, Hugo, 33

Hobbes, Thomas, 11
Homer, 28, 58, 86, 97, 160, 164, 166, 183
Horace, 27, 28, 46–7, 170
Howell, Wilbur Samuel, 3,

10, 15
Hume, David, 6, 15, 23, 43, 52, 53, 88, 89, 100, 104, 105, 112, 139, 140

James, Henry, 180
Johnson, Samuel, 139, 188
Juvenal, 58

Liebniz, Gottfried, 73
Locke, John, 2, 73, 100
Longinus, 62, 94, 98, 132, 157, 159
Lothian, John Maule, 14, 54

Mandeville, Bernard, 11, 65
Manolescu, Beth Innocenti, 13
MacPherson, James, 17, 140
McCosh, James, 180
Massillon, Jean-Baptiste, 173
Mill, James, 179
Mill, John Stuart, 179
Millar, John, 53
Milton, John, 48, 51, 72, 76, 158

Newton, Issac, 2

Oswald, James, 53
Otway, Thomas, 47
Ovid, 149

Quintilian, 6, 61, 63, 86, 98, 123, 125, 126, 134, 168, 169, 171, 178, 182

Peirce, Charles Sanders, 100, 180
Philips, John, 76
Plato, 36, 59, 83
Pope, Alexander, 47, 57–8, 62, 74, 94
Priscian, 137
Pufendorf, Samuel, 33
Pym, John, 59

Robertson, John, 140
Rollin, Charles, 131, 177

Saurin, Joseph, 173
Shaftesbury, Anthony Ashley-Cooper, 3rd Earl of, 59, 60, 68, 72
Shakespeare, 49–50
Sophists, 170, 177
Spencer, Herbert, 179
Stevenson, John, 140
Stewart, John, 15, 111
Suckling, Sir John, 158
Swift, Jonathan, 56, 59, 67, 68, 70–3, 157, 174

Tacitus, 60, 65, 86, 159
Temple, Sir William, 67, 68–70
Turnbull, George, 99

Virgil, 48, 65, 76–87, 160, 164
Vossius, Joannes Gerardus, 177

Waller, Edmund, 59, 158
Warburton, William, 57
Wedderburn, Alexander, 53, 140
Whately, Richard, 18, 184
Witherspoon, John, 6, 139

Xenophon, 84